English

Language acquisition

CAPABLE–PROFICIENT/ PHASES 3–6

Ana de Castro
Zara Kaiserimam
Series editor: Paul Morris

A note about spelling: We have followed IB house style for spelling of certain words, using –ize rather than –ise; and vice versa.

There is a widespread belief that -ize is American English and that British English should use the –ise forms, but for certain verbs/words both endings are correct in British English. The important thing to remember is to be consistent in a piece of writing.

You can find out more information here:
https://www.lexico.com/definition/-ize
https://www.lexico.com/grammar/british-and-spelling

A note about command terms: There are five specific command terms for language acquisition – analyse, evaluate, identify, interpret and synthesize. We have emboldened these five command terms in the book, alongside the wider MYP command terms, so that you familiarise yourself with these terms.

Author's dedication
Ana de Castro – To my parents. Who worked so hard and understood the value of education.

Zara Kaiserimam – To my husband for always listening and my family for having faith in me.
A special thanks to Ana and So-Shan for their kindness and support.

Although every effort has been made to ensure that website addresses are correct at time of going to press, Hodder Education cannot be held responsible for the content of any website mentioned in this book. It is sometimes possible to find a relocated web page by typing in the address of the home page for a website in the URL window of your browser.

Hachette UK's policy is to use papers that are natural, renewable and recyclable products and made from wood grown in well-managed forests and other controlled sources. The logging and manufacturing processes are expected to conform to the environmental regulations of the country of origin.

Orders: please contact Hachette UK Distribution, Hely Hutchinson Centre, Milton Road, Didcot, Oxfordshire, OX11 7HH. Telephone: +44 (0)1235 827827. Email education@hachette.co.uk. Lines are open from 9.00–5.00, Monday to Saturday, with a 24-hour message answering service. You can also order through our website www.hoddereducation.com

© Ana de Castro and Zara Kaiserimam 2016
Revised for the first teaching of MYP Language acquisition 2020
Published by Hodder Education
An Hachette UK Company
Carmelite House, 50 Victoria Embankment, London EC4Y 0DZ

Impression number   5
Year   2021

Cover photo © Robertcicchetti/Thinkstock/iStockphoto/Getty Images
Illustrations by DC Graphic Design Limited
Typeset in Frutiger LT Std 45 Light 11/15pt by DC Graphic Design Limited
Printed in India

A catalogue record for this title is available from the British Library

ISBN 9781471880551

Contents

How to use this book

Welcome to Hodder Education's *MYP by Concept* series! Each chapter is designed to lead you through an *inquiry* into the concepts of Language acquisition, and how they interact in real-life global contexts.

The *Statement of Inquiry* provides the framework for this inquiry, and the *Inquiry questions* then lead us through the exploration as they are developed through each chapter.

Each chapter is framed with a *Key concept*, *Related concept* and set in a *Global context*.

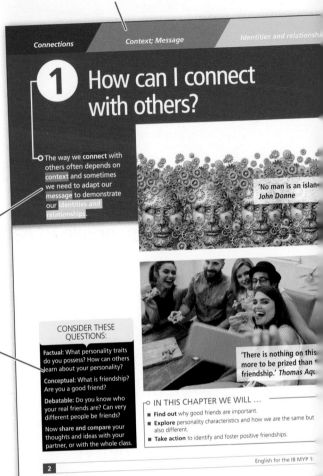

KEY WORDS

Key words are included to give you access to vocabulary for the topic. **Glossary terms** are highlighted and, where applicable, **search terms** are given to encourage independent learning and research skills.

As you explore, activities suggest ways to learn through *action*.

ATL

■ Activities are designed to develop your *Approaches to Learning* (ATL) skills.

EXTENSION

Extension activities allow you to explore a topic further.

◆ **Assessment opportunities in this chapter:**

Some activities are *formative* as they allow you to practise certain parts of the MYP Language acquisition *Assessment Objectives*. Other activities can be used by you or your teachers to assess your achievement against all parts of an assessment objective.

Key *Approaches to Learning* skills for MYP Language acquisition whenever we encounter them.

Hint

In some of the Activities, we provide Hints to help you work on the assignment. This also introduces you to the Hint feature in the on-screen assessment.

ⓘ Definitions are included for important terms and information boxes are included to give background information, more detail and explanation.

At the end of the chapter you are asked to reflect back on what you have learnt with our *Reflection table*, maybe to think of new questions brought to light by your learning.

Use this table to reflect on your own learning in this chapter.					
Questions we asked	Answers we found	Any further questions now?			
Factual					
Conceptual					
Debatable					
Approaches to learning you used in this chapter:	Description – what new skills did you learn?	How well did you master the skills?			
		Novice	Learner	Practitioner	Expert
Learner profile attribute(s)	*Reflect on the importance of the attribute for our learning in this chapter.*				

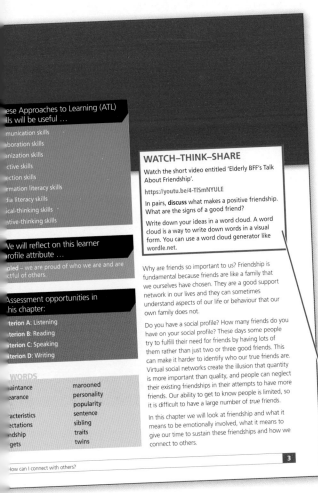

ese Approaches to Learning (ATL)
lls will be useful …

munication skills
aboration skills
anization skills
ctive skills
ection skills
rmation literacy skills
dia literacy skills
ical-thinking skills
ative-thinking skills

We will reflect on this learner
rofile attribute …

pled – we are proud of who we are and are
ctful of others.

Assessment opportunities in
this chapter:

terion A: Listening
terion B: Reading
terion C: Speaking
terion D: Writing

WORDS

aintance   marooned
earance   personality
                popularity
acteristics   sentence
ectations   sibling
ndship   traits
gets   twins

How can I connect with others?   3

WATCH–THINK–SHARE

Watch the short video entitled 'Elderly BFF's Talk About Friendship'.

https://youtu.be/4-TISmNYULE

In pairs, **discuss** what makes a positive friendship. What are the signs of a good friend?

Write down your ideas in a word cloud. A word cloud is a way to write down words in a visual form. You can use a word cloud generator like wordle.net.

Why are friends so important to us? Friendship is fundamental because friends are like a family that we ourselves have chosen. They are a good support network in our lives and they can sometimes understand aspects of our life or behaviour that our own family does not.

Do you have a social profile? How many friends do you have on your social profile? These days some people try to fulfill their need for friends by having lots of them rather than just two or three good friends. This can make it harder to identify who our true friends are. Virtual social networks create the illusion that quantity is more important than quality, and people can neglect their existing friendships in their attempts to have more friends. Our ability to get to know people is limited, so it is difficult to have a large number of *true* friends.

In this chapter we will look at friendship and what it means to be emotionally involved, what it means to give our time to sustain these friendships and how we connect to others.

You are prompted to consider your conceptual understanding in a variety of activities throughout each chapter.

Take action

! While the book provides *opportunities* for action and plenty of content to enrich the conceptual relationships, you must be an active part of this process. Guidance is given to help you with your own research, including how to carry out research, guidance on forming your own research question, as well as linking and developing your study of Language acquisition to the global issues in our twenty-first-century world.

We have incorporated Visible Thinking – ideas, framework, protocol and thinking routines – from Project Zero at the Harvard Graduate School of Education into many of our activities.

▼ Links to:

Like any other subject, Language acquisition is just one part of our bigger picture of the world. Links to other subjects are discussed.

● We will reflect on this learner profile attribute …

Each chapter has an *IB learner profile* attribute as its theme, and you are encouraged to reflect on these too.

1 How can I connect with others?

○ The way we **connect** with others often depends on **context** and sometimes we need to adapt our **message** to demonstrate our **identities and relationships**.

'No man is an island'
John Donne

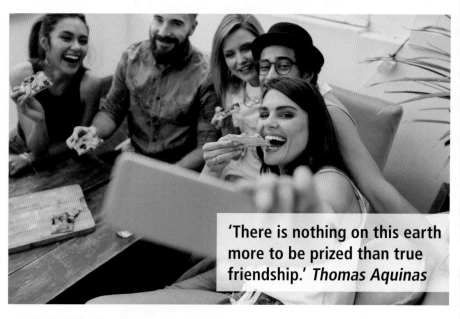

'There is nothing on this earth more to be prized than true friendship.' *Thomas Aquinas*

CONSIDER THESE QUESTIONS:

Factual: What personality traits do you possess? How can others learn about your personality?

Conceptual: What is friendship? Are you a good friend?

Debatable: Do you know who your real friends are? Can very different people be friends?

Now **share and compare** your thoughts and ideas with your partner, or with the whole class.

○ IN THIS CHAPTER WE WILL …

- **Find out** why good friends are important.
- **Explore** personality characteristics and how we are the same but also different.
- **Take action** to identify and foster positive friendships.

■ These Approaches to Learning (ATL) skills will be useful …

- ■ Communication skills
- ■ Collaboration skills
- ■ Organization skills
- ■ Affective skills
- ■ Reflection skills
- ■ Information literacy skills
- ■ Media literacy skills
- ■ Critical-thinking skills
- ■ Creative-thinking skills

● We will reflect on this learner profile attribute …

Principled – we are proud of who we are and are respectful of others.

◆ Assessment opportunities in this chapter:

- ◆ **Criterion A**: Listening
- ◆ **Criterion B**: Reading
- ◆ **Criterion C**: Speaking
- ◆ **Criterion D**: Writing

KEY WORDS

acquaintance	marooned
appearance	personality
BFF	popularity
characteristics	sentence
expectations	sibling
friendship	traits
gadgets	twins

WATCH–THINK–SHARE

Watch the short video entitled 'Elderly BFF's Talk About Friendship'.

https://youtu.be/4-TlSmNYULE

In pairs, **discuss** what makes a positive friendship. What are the signs of a good friend?

Write down your ideas in a word cloud. A word cloud is a way to write down words in a visual form. You can use a word cloud generator like **wordle.net**.

Why are friends so important to us? Friendship is fundamental because friends are like a family that we ourselves have chosen. They are a good support network in our lives and they can sometimes understand aspects of our life or behaviour that our own family does not.

Do you have a social profile? How many friends do you have on your social profile? These days some people try to fulfill their need for friends by having lots of them rather than just two or three good friends. This can make it harder to identify who our true friends are. Virtual social networks create the illusion that quantity is more important than quality, and people can neglect their existing friendships in their attempts to have more friends. Our ability to get to know people is limited, so it is difficult to have a large number of *true* friends.

In this chapter we will look at friendship and what it means to be emotionally involved, what it means to give our time to sustain these friendships and how we connect to others.

What is friendship?

We all have an idea of what a good friend is supposed to be. We make or lose friends because they do or do not live up to our expectations. What has experience taught you about friendship?

Fatima is a very popular girl in her school. She is fun, and gets along with everyone. Fatima has always been friendly and she says hello to everyone. She invites the entire class to her birthday, and occasionally buys gifts for everyone. She is usually busy with her many friends, but finds that she sometimes has very little time to be with all of them because she knows so many people. It is not easy to decide who to be with at times. She is the girl with most friends at school and in her neighbourhood.

One day it all changes.

The teacher decides to celebrate friendship day. She asks the students to make gifts for three special friends to share with at the end of the day. Everyone is excited. Fatima thinks she is very lucky because she has so many friends to choose from.

Everyone finishes and they give each other their gifts, but Fatima does not receive any! Fatima looks very sad and confused.

A lot of research has been carried out looking at the benefits of friendship, and this has found exactly what you might expect. It turns out that the better quality relationships you have, the more likely you are to be happy! Therefore it's good for your happiness to be a great friend to someone and to have a group of good friends supporting you. But it can be difficult to identify what makes a good friend.

'How is it possible? I put so much effort into having so many friends, and it turns out that no one thinks of me as their best friend!'

Fatima thinks that she is a good classmate and she knows many people. She tries not to upset anyone or make anyone angry but now understands that this means that she does not really get to know anyone deeply.

So, she goes home in floods of tears and asks her mother where she can get real friends. Fatima's mother explains gently that you cannot buy friendship. She explains that to find true friends you have to be prepared to be there for your friends in good times and bad times. Fatima finds this difficult to understand as she wants to be friends with everyone. Her mother tries to explain the difference between a true friend and an acquaintance, and how you can only have a handful of true friends because you need to spend quality time with them.

'Think about people who really love you. What do they do to be there for you?'

■ The friendship between Woody and Buzz in *Toy Story* was not perfect at the start. The characters are quite different from one another and theirs is an unlikely friendship

ACTIVITY: Friends or acquaintances?

Task 1

Read the text on page 4 and answer the questions.

1 **Identify** the type of text this is.
2 What kind of person is Fatima?
3 **Evaluate** if friendship is important to Fatima. Why? Why not?
4 Fatima has a lot of free time. True or false? **Quote** words from the text to **justify** your answer.
5 Why is Fatima excited?
6 What is the penultimate paragraph (which begins, 'So, she goes home …') about? **Summarize** it in one sentence.
7 Find one word that means 'regularly'.
8 What does Fatima not understand? Why is she upset?
9 What is the difference between a friend and an acquaintance?

Task 2

Read the text again.

In pairs, write the word FRIENDSHIP down the left-hand side of a page. Now write a sentence, phrase or special word about friendship and friends starting with each of the letters of the word. Use a new idea for each letter.

You have created an **acrostic** poem! An acrostic poem is made by using each letter from a word to write ideas and feelings that are connected to that word. Read your FRIENDSHIP poem to your class.

Task 3

Who is your best friend? Think about what makes your friend unique and special. Think about the similarities and differences between you. Think about your friend's hobbies, interests, things that they are good at, feelings, family and friends and personality.

Try writing an acrostic poem using the letters of your best friend's name.

ACTIVITY: Who am I?

Use a search engine and look for the IB learner profile attributes.

Prepare a PowerPoint presentation made up of simple sentences about you. Choose the IB learner profile attributes that best fits you. Present and **describe** yourself to your classmates.

Prepare pictures to support your oral presentation about yourself. You should plan to speak for about one minute.

What personality traits do I possess?

HOW CAN OTHERS LEARN ABOUT MY PERSONALITY?

Have you ever stopped to people-watch? Have you noticed how everyone is different? We are similar in so many ways and yet in other ways we are all unique. We all have the same human nature and we share a common humanity but no two people are truly alike. No two people can ever have the same experience of life or the same perspective, that is, the same way of looking at things.

We have different ideas about things; we feel in different ways and we behave differently too. This is what makes a person unique. Even twins will experience things in their own individual way.

Our experiences, along with our human characteristics, shape our personalities. Even our families and friends contribute to our personalities. These personality traits make us who we are.

EXTENSION

Have you ever taken a personality test? Use the internet to search for some fun personality tests and try them!

Discuss what you can tell about a person from their answers on a personality test. Do you think that these types of personality quizzes are accurate?

ACTIVITY: What do we mean by personality?

■ ATL

Reflection skills: Develop new skills, techniques and strategies for effective learning; demonstrate flexibility in the selection and use of learning strategies

Organization skills: Use appropriate strategies for organizing complex information

Task 1

Match the words below to the descriptions that follow.

brave	caring	clever	generous
hard-working	honest	humorous	rude
shy	tidy		

- **Someone who is a risk-taker.**
- **Someone who shares things with others.**
- **A person who can see the funny side of things.**
- **Someone who is kind to others.**
- **A person with bad manners.**
- **A person who always completes tasks and is committed.**
- **Someone who tells the truth and is reliable.**
- **A person who finds learning easy.**
- **Someone who puts things back in their place.**
- **A person who finds it difficult to talk to people.**

Task 2

In pairs, look at the list of words on the opposite page. They are personality **adjectives**. **Identify** if they are negative or positive characteristics.

Think about how you can record new words to help you learn new vocabulary. Look at the information box on page 8 for ideas.

Task 3

In pairs, **describe** the character of the famous people in the photographs. You can use words from the previous task or come up with your own.

■ Roger Federer, an inspiration to young tennis players

■ Stephen Hawking, English theoretical physicist and cosmologist

■ Aung San Suu Kyi, activist and opposition leader in her home country Burma

■ Amelia Earhart, American aviation pioneer and author

Task 4

In pairs, each think of another famous person. Use personality adjectives to **describe** the person until your partner can guess who you are talking about. Carry on thinking of different people and see who guesses the most!

◆ **Assessment opportunities**

In this activity you have practised skills that are assessed using Criterion C: Speaking.

affectionate	aggressive	big-headed	boring	bossy	careless	communicative
cowardly	creative	cruel	determined	dishonest	easygoing	energetic
enthusiastic	friendly	gentle	good	greedy	grumpy	helpful
imaginative	impatient	impolite	impulsive	inconsiderate	independent	intelligent
intolerant	inventive	irresponsible	jealous	kind	lazy	loving
loyal	mean	moody	narrow-minded	nervous	nice	open-minded
optimistic	overcritical	overemotional	passionate	patient	pessimistic	polite
possessive	powerful	practical	quick-tempered	reliable	resentful	rude
secretive	selfish	sensible	sensitive	silly	stingy	stubborn
stupid	superficial	sympathetic	thoughtful	thoughtless	tidy	timid
understanding	unkind	unreliable	untidy	untrustworthy	witty	

How to learn vocabulary

When it comes to learning a new language, vocabulary is key. But what can we do to help ourselves learn and remember new words?

Finding a strategy or a combination of strategies to help us organize words is important. You may be surprised to find that the best way to learn new words is by reading! The more you read, the more words you will discover. When you read lots of different things you can learn words linked to a wider range of topics, such as sport, fashion and film.

Look at these strategies that you can use to help you learn and remember words. Connecting words to your own experience will make them more meaningful.

Decide which of these strategies to use for different topics or school subjects.

Word lists: Write down words you learn (with or without translations). Remember to go over your list often so you don't forget the words.

Group words: It can be a good idea to group words around a central topic or idea, for example, animals, family, hobbies and interests, and school life. This can help you to develop your speaking skills and share your ideas about important topics.

Synonyms and antonyms: A synonym is a word that has the *same* meaning; an antonym is a word that means the *opposite*. For example, *big* and *huge* are synonyms; *big* and *small* are antonyms. When you learn a new word, learning its synonyms and antonyms will build up your vocabulary quickly.

Picture it: Visualize words by creating your own picture word lists.

Colour code it: Use colours to help you to remember how to use and when to use words. For example, use different colours for different tenses, or different parts of speech, such as adjectives, nouns and so on.

Word games: Crossword puzzles, word searches and other language games will help you to build your vocabulary while you have fun.

Use what you know: As soon as you learn a new word, start using it. Use it in your own speaking and writing. Using new words in your daily vocabulary will help you to remember and become more fluent.

Repetition, repetition: Researchers say you must see and hear a word 10–20 times for it to become part of your vocabulary. Don't worry if you forget a word you once knew. If you keep reading and hearing the word, you will eventually learn it!

ACTIVITY: *The Boy in the Striped Pyjamas*

The Boy in the Striped Pyjamas is a novel by John Boyne. It has also been adapted into a film.

How do you say the *The Boy in the Striped Pyjamas* in your language?

Watch the trailer for the film: **https://youtu.be/9ypMp0s5Hiw**.

In pairs, write down the personality traits for the following characters:

- **Bruno, who has moved to the countryside**
- **Shmuel, who is in the concentration camp**
- **Mother**
- **Father**

In pairs, **discuss** how the family is presented in the film. How is friendship presented in the film? How is Bruno's friendship with Shmuel different from the one that he has with his friends in the city?

If you haven't read the book, why not borrow it from your library and read it in your own language or in English? You won't be disappointed!

■ 'Bruno was sure that he had never seen a skinnier or sadder boy in his life but decided that he had better talk to him.' *The Boy in the Striped Pyjamas* by John Boyne

How to summarize a text

Learning how to extract the main ideas and points from a text is very important and it will help you to make good notes for all your MYP subjects.

Follow these simple steps to summarize a text:
- **Identify** the key information in the text.
- Highlight the words that give this key information – just three to five words.
- Look at each paragraph and highlight or underline the main sentence – this is usually the first sentence in the paragraph, but it can also be another one. It will make the most important point that is then extended in the paragraph.
- Remember to use only your key points to write your summary.

Reflection skills: Develop new skills, techniques and strategies for effective learning

Communication skills: Give and receive meaningful feedback

Task

Read the article opposite.

In pairs, choose a strategy to use to learn any new vocabulary from the text. Remember you can use more than one strategy.

THINK–PAIR–SHARE

Read the text again and make notes on the main reason Jorge Fernández wants to spend the weekend in the Rocky Mountains.

Using the notes you have just made, **summarize** the article in approximately 100 words.

Share your article with your partner and give each other feedback.

Where would you like to spend your weekend?

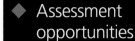

Assessment opportunities

In this activity you have practised skills that are assessed using Criterion B: Reading.

A weekend to remember!

■ Columbine flowers, the symbol for Colorado

This weekend I would love to be walking and climbing in the Rocky Mountains in Colorado with my dogs Daisy and Ollie. I went there four years ago with my sister, who is also my best friend. It was spectacular, with amazing wildflowers and the brightest blue sky you have ever seen. And I would love to go again!

The local people in a nearby town called Nederland, say that once you've hiked in the Rockies you just want to become a mountaineer! You can climb up into the high country full of moose and wild cats. It is old mining country and you come across evidence of the old miners everywhere.

It is a great place to go on your own or with anyone who has a love for the outdoor life. You can take a local guide to explore the natural habitat and he or she can teach you about the rocks and minerals Colorado is famous for.

The whole place is full of lakes, glaciers and wildlife and the local people, the mountain people, are very friendly. There are many hikes that you can do, some easier and some quite challenging. There is one thing that can be annoying and that is that you have to stick to the paths and you cannot let your dogs run loose! It is a National Park and there are strict rules to protect the environment.

It is a wonderful place to visit with friends too. You can choose to spend a night in the mountains up by the lakes and you can find cabins for shelter. You need to take lots of water and cereal bars for energy. Some people find the altitude difficult and it does take time to get used to it when hiking.

I intend to go back to the area next year, and I will climb one of the highest peaks! It really is magical, and just thinking about it today makes me want to be there right now.

Jorge Fernández

ACTIVITY: What do the things I like say about me?

■ ATL

Communication skills: Structure information in summaries, essays and reports

Have you heard of Robinson Crusoe? He is the **protagonist** of a story written by Daniel Defoe about a man who is marooned, that is, trapped with no way to leave, on a desert island and spends a long time living on his own until he meets another human being, called Friday.

Task 1

Imagine you are marooned on a desert island. Choose five things you would want to have with you. Write a few words to **describe** your items.

Task 2

You are now going to develop these ideas into a paragraph.

Remember that several sentences together about one topic make a paragraph, and that each sentence must have a verb, subject and object.

Hint

Have a look at this website for more information on how to write good sentences:
www.bbc.co.uk/education/guides/zpqnfg8/revision

Choose from the words below to help you write your sentences. You can add words of your own.

Start your paragraph like this:

If I were marooned on a desert island, I would want these things with me.

This is because I am …

artistic	book-mad	caring
friendly	a homebody	interested in film
love gadgets	musical	reserved
sociable	sporty	a thinker

◆ Assessment opportunities

In this activity you have practised skills that are assessed using Criterion D: Writing.

Let's talk grammar

Subject: the person or thing a sentence is about.

For example: *Ludovic plays basketball*

      (subject)   **(object)**

Object: the person or thing affected by the sentence's verb.

For example: *They watch television*.

    (subject) (verb) (object)

Verb: a word that expresses the action of a person or thing. Always remember to check the tense. For example, run, talk, play, see, go are all verbs.

Simple sentence: a group of words that includes a verb and makes complete sense.

For example: *I live in Lima. He goes to school.*

ℹ Did you know that the original title of Defoe's novel *Robinson Crusoe* was 'The Life and Strange Surprising Adventures of Robinson Crusoe, of York, Mariner: Who Lived Eight and Twenty Years, All Alone in an Un-inhabited Island on the Coast of America, Near the Mouth of the Great River of Oroonoque; Having Been Cast on Shore by Shipwreck, Wherein All the Men Perished but Himself. With an Account how he was at last as Strangely Deliver'd by Pyrates. Written by Himself.'

In pairs or groups of three, use a search engine to carry out some research about other **unusual titles for books**. Or just find out more about the **oddest stories**. What did you learn?

In your pairs or groups, present the information to your class. Don't be afraid to include pictures.

Seeing double

Can you imagine what it's like to have a sibling with the same birthday as you, who looks just like you, and shares everything with you? Well, I found out the answers to these questions when I talked to identical twins Alejandra and Maria.

NATHAN: I think what our readers are interested to know is, what's it like being twins?

ALEJANDRA: I don't mind being a twin … most of the time. But there are good things and bad things. Maria and I both have blonde hair, though of course I've got a fringe. We know that our appearance is similar and people are always looking at us.

MARIA: We have very pale skin and hundreds of freckles, and we both absolutely hate them. Neither of us can sunbathe nor spend much time in the sun, because we both always burn really easily.

NATHAN: You're both very similar physically but what else is the same?

ALEJANDRA: Friends ask me if Maria and I know what each of us is thinking or if we feel the same things. As strange as this sounds, we do! It happened all the time when we were little and it still happens now. When one of us has a headache, the other twin gets one too. When I feel sick, I'm never surprised to hear that Maria feels ill too. This happens even when we are not together.

NATHAN: How interesting! What other things do you have in common?

MARIA: We often finish each other's sentences when we're talking. It can be annoying at times! I think it's because identical twins have almost identical brain activity. Many twins have a language that only they use. When Alejandra and I were younger, we had our own language too. But we're using it less and less these days. I think we are spending less time with each other too.

NATHAN: And in what ways do you think you are different from each other?

ALEJANDRA: I'm not as outgoing as Maria and I like to stay at home more.

MARIA: That's not true! You are just as talkative as I am.

ALEJANDRA: It is true. I'm quieter and find it harder to make friends at school. I love sports and I like to wear casual, comfortable clothes, but Maria is more creative and artistic. She is more into fashion than I am. She loves going to parties and is more sociable.

MARIA: There's nothing wrong with liking fashionable clothes, especially dresses, and I love wearing high heels! I do like to have fun and spend time with my friends but I love to be with my twin too!

ALEJANDRA: And I hate wearing dresses, so people know who is who!

NATHAN: That's great! Thank you for sharing your experiences.

Nathan Jenkins

PERSONOLOGY

Did you know that face reading is also called personology? Some people believe that your face is the mirror of your personality and there are statistical results which show that there is a strong connection between facial features and personality traits. The results of one study indicates that 90 per cent of us think we know what a person is like by looking at their face.

For thousands of years people have been trying to study the relationship between facial features and personality traits. Reading people's faces or having an understanding of body language is linked to emotional intelligence. Some people believe you can become more successful by developing these skills.

What do you think? Is it a useful skill to have?

▼ Links to: Science

There is research that links personality to **genes**. Carry out your own research to consider if character is something you are born with or if it is developed. Can someone change their personality?

Make a note of the resources you have consulted and put together a PowerPoint with the most important ideas you have found.

Here are two articles to help you get started. www.telegraph.co.uk/news/science/science-news/9267147/Its-nature-not-nurture-personality-lies-in-genes-twins-study-shows.html

https://www.psychologytoday.com/ blog/under-the-influence/201307/do-genes-influence-personality

Why not organize a class discussion on the topic?

ACTIVITY: Seeing double

■ ATL

Reflection skills: Focus on the process of creating by imitating the work of others

Communication skills: Paraphrase accurately and concisely

Task 1

- **What type of text is 'Seeing double'?**
- **Identify how the twins are similar.**
- **Identify how they are different.**
- **Do they like being twins? Why? Why not?**
- **Interpret how people react to the twins.**

Task 2

In the text there are many examples of sentences in the **present simple** tense (an example would be: *She has brown eyes*) and **present continuous** tense (an example would be: *He is wearing trousers*). Individually, copy and complete the rules for the present simple and the present continuous.

We use the _____ for:

- **routines and habits**
- **things that are always true**
- **scientific facts.**

We use the _____ for:

- **things happening now**
- **temporary actions**
- **annoying actions**
- **changing situations.**

Now look at the text again and **identify** sentences that are in the present simple and present continuous.

Task 3

Do you have a brother or sister? Would you like to be a twin? Write another 100–150-word paragraph about your sibling or a relative. Write sentences using the present simple and the present continuous.

◆ Assessment opportunities

In this activity you have practised skills that are assessed using Criterion B: Reading and Criterion D: Writing.

ACTIVITY: What's in a face?

■ ATL

Information literacy skills: Make connections between various sources of information

Communication skills: Interpret and use effectively modes of non-verbal communication

Task 1

Take a short quiz to find out how good you are at reading people: **http://greatergood.berkeley.edu/ei_quiz/**. How many expressions did you guess?

Share your score with your classmates. Do you think this is a good way to judge what a person is like? Is it scientific?

Task 2

In pairs, visit the following website: **www.wikihow.com/Read-Faces**. Make notes on how to read people's facial expressions.

Now listen to the short video clip posted in the *New Scientist* and add to your notes: **www.scienceofpeople.com/2013/09/guide-reading-microexpressions/**.

Task 3

In groups of three, design your own quiz to see how good students are at judging what a person is like. Choose photographs of famous people and write a personality description for each image. Use your notes and the ideas from the websites you have visited.

You can also use a quiz generator website to help you, for example: **www.onlinequizcreator.com**.

◆ Assessment opportunities

In this activity you have practised skills that are assessed using Criterion A: Listening.

Do you know who your real friends are?

DISCUSS

Why do I get along with some people more than I do with others? Who do I trust?

Have you told a friend something that they didn't keep to themselves? Sometimes personal information is only shared between close friends – but sometimes a friend can go behind your back and spill the beans (in other words, share the information with others). Has this happened to you? What do you do when you think your trust has been broken?

Building relationships is not just about making friendships. Relationships can be built through activities or events that lead to something good. One of the best ways to develop relationships with people is to do activities together, for example, play games. Many companies believe this is true and they organize team-building activities for their employees. It seems that the older we get the more difficult it is to have friendships. Children and young people are usually more willing to let people into their world, and less likely to prejudge people.

ACTIVITY: Control tower

◼ ATL

Collaboration skills: Exercise leadership and take on a variety of roles within groups

Have a go at playing the trust game, control tower.

Start by creating an obstacle course in your classroom. In pairs, you will take turns being blindfolded (having your eyes covered so you cannot see) while your partner guides you through the obstacle course. When you have successfully reached the end of the course, change the course and swap roles.

When you have had your turn, write a paragraph to **describe** how it felt to be guided through the course by your partner. What skills did your partner use to get you through the obstacle course?

◆ Assessment opportunities

In this activity you have practised skills that are assessed using Criterion D: Writing.

ACTIVITY: Young people in the media

◼ ATL

Media literacy: Demonstrate awareness of media interpretations of events and ideas (including digital social media)

In groups of three, collect images of teenagers from magazines, newspapers and other media. Look at any headlines that involve teenagers.

Using key words from your research **create** a collage that **describes** society's perception of youth – how it sees young people.

Discuss whether the key words are positive or negative. What stereotypes of teenagers did you find? How do you feel about the images of young people that you see in the media? What images of young people do you find in school? How are young people making friends in social media?

◆ Assessment opportunities

In this activity you have practised skills that are assessed using Criterion C: Speaking.

THINK–PAIR–SHARE

■ ATL

Creative-thinking skills: Use brainstorming and visual diagrams to generate new ideas and inquiries

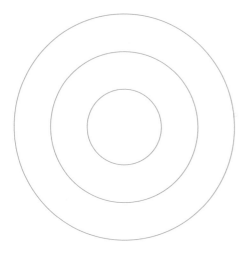

In a copy of the diagram above, you are going to list all your friends.

Put your best friends in the circle in the centre.

In the outer circles put your other friends, people in your class you get on with and finally your acquaintances.

In pairs, **discuss** how your friendships have changed since you started your school. Has this been easy or difficult for you?

◆ Assessment opportunities

In this activity you have practised skills that are assessed using Criterion C: Speaking.

WATCH–PAIR–SHARE

■ ATL

Collaboration skills: Practise empathy

Affective skills: Practise dealing with change

Watch the video clip about balancing longstanding friendships and relationships: https://www.bbc.co.uk/programmes/p068t62w.

Consider the following questions:
- **What is the purpose of the video?**
- **Identify** how the creator of the video makes the video engaging.
- **Summarise** the most surprising or interesting thing you learnt from the video.

In pairs, or groups of three, **discuss** the following:
- **Identify** how Eli feels.
- **Interpret** how Joe feels.
- **Has anything like this happened to you?**
- **Evaluate** how you could deal with this in a positive way.
- **Identify** the difference between a friend and an acquaintance.
- **Interpret** how you tell the difference between a true friend and a false friend.
- **What is a 'best friend'?**
- **Can you have more than one best friend? Why? Why not?**
- **Analyse** the difference between popularity and friendship.

◆ Assessment opportunities

In this activity you have practised skills that are assessed using Criterion A: Listening.

ACTIVITY: BFF

■ ATL

Communication skills: Use intercultural understanding to interpret communication

Affective skills: Practise dealing with disappointment and unmet expectations

Discuss with a partner what you think BFF stands for. Do you use different expressions when you are talking to your friends? Do you speak to your family in the same way? Why? Why not?

Listen to the song 'What About Your Friends' by TLC: www.youtube.com/watch?v=2436DSTOYo4.

The song came out in 1992 shortly after TLC became famous.

Read the lyrics to the song: www.lyricsfreak.com/t/tlc/what+about+your+friends_10232717.html.

Consider the following questions:
- **What is the purpose of the song?**
- **Identify** how the singer feels about her friends.
- **Summarize** the message in the song.

Now listen again and write down some of the colloquial expressions in the song. Colloquial expressions are informal language used when we speak. In pairs, look at your examples and using your own words **explain** what the phrases mean.

How would you say these expressions in your language? Was the song difficult to understand? Why? Why not?

◆ Assessment opportunities

In this activity you have practised skills that are assessed using Criterion A: Listening.

WATCH–PAIR–SHARE

■ ATL

Critical-thinking skills: Revise understanding based on new information and evidence

Affective skills: Practise positive thinking

Watch the TEDxYouth talk by Catalina Ritzinger entitled 'Friendship and Family': www.youtube.com/watch?v=Bug8fAZdh5s.

Consider the following questions:
- **What is the purpose of the video?**
- **Identify** how the creator of the video makes the video engaging.
- **Summarise** the most surprising or interesting thing you learnt from the video.

In pairs, **discuss** the following questions:
- **When does Catalina say you know who your true friends are?**
- **Who does Catalina say she can rely on?**
- **Evaluate** how Catalina says she used to behave when she got home from school.
- **Identify** what Catalina says she thought was the most important thing for her at that time.
- **What does Catalina identify** as being normal behaviour when you are a teenager?
- **Identify** the two 'defining moments'.
- **What are the words that Catalina uses to describe people who are not really friends? What does she say they do?**
- **Summarize** how she describes her best friend.
- **What promises did Catalina's BFF make to her?**
- **Evaluate** how these promises made Catalina feel.
- **What happened to their friendship?**
- Write a sentence to **explain** what Catalina finally understood about friends.
- **Identify** who she says her true friends are.
- **Explain** in your own words what 'they have your back' means.

◆ Assessment opportunities

In this activity you have practised skills that are assessed using Criterion A: Listening.

TED Talks are videos in which speakers present great, well-formed ideas in under 18 minutes. They are shared through the TED organization. There are seven different types of talks that you can access and the talks can be used to highlight and present ideas to a wide range of audiences. They usually focus on relevant and current topics and, as they are under 18 minutes long, it is easy to remember the main points.

TEDxYouth events are fun, imaginative and often organized by young people.

A TEDx Talk is an independently organized event that anyone can run after gaining a licence from TED.

A **fable** is a short tale, often with animals as characters, which teaches a moral lesson.

READ–THINK–SHARE

■ Fables are important because they teach valuable lessons about life, in a humorous yet interesting way

In previous tasks in this chapter, you have considered the qualities of a good friend. But are all our friends good for us? Is it possible for a friend to lead us down a path we might regret later? Can we call people who are encouraging us to behave badly or take risks real friends?

Task 1

Read these two Aesop fables about friendship and **summarize** in two sentences what each fable is about. Share your ideas with your partner.

www.taleswithmorals.com/aesop-fable-the-hare-with-many-friends.htm

www.taleswithmorals.com/aesop-fable-the-lion-and-the-mouse.htm

Task 2

In pairs, write your own fable about friendship in the style of the Aesop's tales you have just looked at. Remember that a lesson must be learnt from your tale.

ACTIVITY: Can you choose your friends?

Look at these words and place them in order of importance for making a good friend.

clever	exciting	fashionable
funny	friendly	gets into trouble
honest	kind	likes school work
likes similar things		
listens to your problems		
loyal	popular	reliable
shares	sticks up for you	
supportive	talks behind your back	
trusting	wants you to impress them	

In pairs, **discuss** how having good relationships or friendships with people can help you cope better with the stresses and challenges of life.

In groups, **discuss** when you have experienced someone being loyal or disloyal, when you have had a friend who has listened or not listened, and when a friend has given you good or bad advice.

◆ Assessment opportunities

In this activity you have practised skills that are assessed using Criterion C: Speaking.

ACTIVITY: Role play

In groups of four, **create** a role play for the scenarios opposite and **discuss** how you should and shouldn't react in these circumstances. Everyone in the team should have a role within the play. Take turns to act out your role play to the class.

Role play 1 – One of you has fallen out within a group of friends.

Role play 2 – A friend calls you boring because you won't join in.

Role play 3 – A friend keeps making excuses when you ask them to meet you.

Role play 4 – A friend stops talking to you after you won the maths prize in school.

Role play 5 – A friend from primary school has made some new friends and they don't include you in their new friendships.

Role play 6 – You find out there is going to be a party but you haven't been invited.

Role play 7 – One of your friends wants you to exclude someone you get on with. They have told you that if you don't do what they say, they will stop talking to you.

Evaluate the role plays and then give feedback to each group after performing the role play.

What is a multimodal text?

We don't just use language to communicate ideas; images, whether still or moving, can be combined with text to convey messages or to present arguments.

Texts which consist of more than one mode, for instance texts which make use of both written and visual modes, are called **multimodal texts**.

Comic books are a great example of this as they not only use pictures and texts to create narratives, but also include spoken language elements which can make the texts more accessible for readers.

Can you think of any other types of texts which can be considered multimodal? Use the internet to carry out some research and compile your own list of multimodal text types.

▼ Links to: Individuals and societies; Language and literature; Arts

The theme of friendship, friends and relationships has inspired some of the most beautiful poems and stories. Bonds of friendship can be formed in many different ways such as through sharing common interests and challenges, or even geographical proximity. Some of the most striking friendships are as a result of opposites attracting!

Research and find out about some of these unlikely friendships in history and the arts. Write a paragraph about their friendship and highlight why it was unusual.

ACTIVITY: Take the quiz!

Critical-thinking skills: Draw reasonable conclusions and generalizations

Individually, look at the quiz below and answer the questions.

What things do you need to be able to do to make changing friendships less stressful for each other? How can you look after each other?

1 Some friends dare you to do something dangerous that could have serious consequences. Do you:
   a Agree to do it because you don't want to lose their friendship.
   b Make up an excuse for not doing it.
   c Say no and say you don't want to do anything dangerous.

2 Two of your friends have an argument. Do you:
   a Decide to support your favourite friend.
   b Not get involved and let your friends find a solution to their problem.
   c Listen to both of them and support who you think is in the right.

3 Your friends are talking about relationships in a way that makes you uncomfortable. Do you:
   a Participate in the conversation, although you are unhappy about it.
   b Not say anything at all.
   c Speak up and let them know how you think.

4 You see a group of friends being mean and saying nasty things to another student. Do you:
   a Start making mean comments too, so that you do not feel left out.
   b Not say anything, but not stop them either.
   c Ask them to stop and tell them why.

5 One of your friends asks you to lie for them to stop them getting into trouble at school. Do you:
   a Agree to lie because you don't want them to stop being friends with you.
   b Agree but only if what they have done is not serious or dangerous.

   c Refuse and let your friend know it is not OK to get involved with things that affect them and school.

6 You are with a friend and they say something you do not agree with. Do you:
   a Agree in order to avoid an argument.
   b Give your opinion when they ask you what you think.
   c Tell them you don't agree and explain why.

7 You have made friends with someone outside your group. Your friends do not like them. Do you:
   a Stop being friends with the new person.
   b Ask your friends to tell you why they do not like them and make up your own mind.
   c Tell them they can't tell you what to do and that you'll choose your own friends.

8 Your friends ask you to do something that may get you in trouble with the police. Do you:
   a Do it because everyone else is.
   b Talk to them to try and get them to change their minds because you know it is wrong, but do it if they do not change their minds.
   c Say no and walk away.

9 Your friends ask you to smoke a cigarette. You don't smoke. They have told you that nobody will find out. Do you:
   a Smoke. Nobody will find out after all.
   b Ask your friends if they know smoking is bad for you, but smoke anyway.
   c Say no and tell them about the health problems of smoking.

10 Your best friend has had a tattoo done. Your parents have forbidden you from getting one. Your best friend tells you that if you don't get it done it will mean that you are not loyal to them and they will never speak to you again. Do you:
   a Have a small tattoo done where your parents won't see it.
   b Make a health excuse for not getting one.
   c Tell your friend that you don't think a tattoo is evidence of your loyalty and refuse to get one.

Now check your answers ...

Answers mostly A

Your friends are very important to you and you worry about what they think about you. You will do anything not to lose your friends. This means that you do not make your own decisions or choices but will decide to do things they want you to do. You need to stop and think about what you want and how you want to behave and not worry about trying to please your friends.

Answers mostly B

You do not always know what decisions to make and are unsure of yourself, especially as you do not want to upset your friends. You look for excuses and ways to not have to make a decision. It is important that you start to believe in yourself and be prepared to say what you think, even if this means that others might not like what they hear.

Answers mostly C

You know who you are and are not afraid to say what you think. You are confident and know what is right and wrong and you know that sometimes this will cause problems with your friends but it is more important to act according to your principles. You have true friends who accept you for who you are and you will not be pushed to do anything you do not want to do.

! Take action

! Organize a Friendship Assembly in school. The assembly on friendships will provide an opportunity to explore the concept of friendships and encourage you to consider and reflect upon your own relationships.

! The UN International Day of Friendship focuses on involving young people in community activities that include different cultures and promote international understanding. Find ways of promoting Friendship Day within your school community to promote international understanding.

> Did you know that on 27 April 2011 the General Assembly of the United Nations declared **30 July** as official International Friendship Day? However, some countries, including India, celebrate Friendship Day on the **first Sunday of August**.

! Take a look at this website for further ideas: **www.friendship.com.au/friendday.html**.

! Write poems to celebrate Friendship Day. Look at this website for ideas: **www.friendshipday.org/friendship-day-poems.html**.

! Go beyond the classroom and think about the theme of friendship around the world by focusing on relations between countries.

◆ Assessment opportunities

In this activity you have practised skills that are assessed using Criterion B: Reading.

SOME SUMMATIVE TASKS TO TRY

Use these tasks to apply and extend your learning in this chapter. These tasks are designed so that you can evaluate your learning in the Language acquisition criteria.

THIS TASK CAN BE USED TO EVALUATE YOUR LEARNING IN CRITERION C TO CAPABLE LEVEL

Task 1: Interactive oral

■ You will engage in a discussion with the teacher on friendship.
■ Look at the images below.
■ You are expected to speak for 3–4 minutes.

1 The two images are identical. True or false?
2 Describe in three sentences what you see in the images.
3 Describe what the girl in the first image feels for her friends. What makes you think so?
4 **Identify** how old the people in the pictures are.
5 **Analyse** the purpose of the images.
6 Do you like the colours in the images? Why? Why not?
7 **Evaluate** how well the images portray friendships. Justify your answer.
8 How is your best friend similar to or different from you?

Task 2: Reading comprehension

- Read the text below and look at the accompanying images.
- Answer the questions that follow, using your own words as much as possible.
- Dictionaries are not allowed to be used in this task.
- Refer as closely as possible to the text, justifying your answers and giving examples when asked.
- You have 60 minutes to complete this task.

Alya has a busy week

Alya lives in Helsinki although she was born in Fez. She is a very busy student! She has a lot of hobbies and interests.

She usually gets up early so she can do her chores before going to school. She doesn't often have time to ski, but she sometimes goes skiing on Saturdays during the winter. Alya often rides a horse at a stable near her home. She finishes school at 15.15 on Friday so she goes to the stable in the afternoon.

Alya goes to an international school, which she enjoys because she loves learning and there are so many great activities to do. She does many extra-curricular activities and tries to participate as much as she can in her school community. She doesn't have much free time, so she rarely goes out during the week.

She seldom watches TV because she likes doing things outside. When the weather is bad she loves to go swimming. She isn't often alone because she has a lot of close friends. On Saturdays and Sundays she meets her friends and they either go out for hot chocolate or go to the cinema. Alya agrees that she is a busy but happy young woman!

1 **Identify** the sports Alya does in the winter.   (strand i)
2 Alya does not like school. True or false?   (strand i)
   Quote words from the text to justify your answer:
   '_____'   (strand i)
3 When does Alya go swimming?   (strand i)
4 Find a word/s in the text that is/are similar to:
   - practising
   - hardly ever.   (strand i)

5 What is the last paragraph about? **Summarize** it in one sentence. (strand ii)

6 Find two words that mean 'regularly'. (strand i)

7 Do you agree with the title of this text? Explain why. (strand ii)

8 What is the purpose of this text? (strand ii)

9 Is Alya sad that she rarely goes out during the week? Why? Support your answer with examples from the text. (strand i)

10 **Interpret** why Alya is so happy in her school. (strand i)

11 How do you know that Alya doesn't feel lonely? (strand i)

12 Does Alya like watching TV? Support your answer with examples from the text. (strand i)

13 What kind of text is it? (strand i)

14 Do you know anyone like Alya? (strand iii)

15 How are you similar to or different from Alya? (strand iii)

THIS TASK CAN BE USED TO EVALUATE YOUR LEARNING IN CRITERION D TO CAPABLE LEVEL

Task 3: Me, myself and I

■ Follow the link and read the article. Now read the prompt and use the images from the article as inspiration to produce your own yearbook entry. https://www.shutterfly.com/ideas/what-to-write-in-a-yearbook/

■ Do not use translating devices or dictionaries for this task.

■ You will have 60 minutes to complete this task.

Describe yourself, your personality traits and your hobbies for your school's yearbook.

■ Write 200–250 words.

THIS TASK CAN BE USED TO EVALUATE YOUR LEARNING IN CRITERION A TO CAPABLE LEVEL

Task 4: Conversation between friends

■ Watch the video clip.

■ Answer the following questions and use your own words as much as possible.

■ Dictionaries are not allowed to be used in this task.

■ Answer the questions in English.

■ You have 60 minutes to complete this task.

https://youtu.be/URJubWfOPtI?list=PLwuNbpP-tqNUFaX-8f1N-bgBufodfhGXD

1 What is this text about? (strand i)

2 Identify the type of text it is (strand ii)
   ■ a blog
   ■ a video
   ■ a website.

3 **Identify** the title of the text. (strand ii)

4 How many people are there in the text? (strand ii)

5 How long is the text? (strand ii)

6 Who made the text? (strand ii)

7 What is the purpose of the text? (strand i)

8 **Identify** how long they have been best friends for. (strand ii)

9 Why do you think their friendship is special? (strand iii)

10 Do you have a best friend? What is your best friend called? (strand iii)

11 Do you prefer to have one best friend or many different friends? (strand iii)

12 Do you like this video? Why? Why not? (strand iii)

Reflection

In this chapter we have seen how friendships are an important part of life that shape our **identities and relationships**. They can help us get through the difficult times and be there for the fun parts too. Making and keeping friends is not always easy. We also need to realize that not all friendships are positive and that there is a danger of not recognizing potentially damaging friendships and associations. Friendship is based on trust and consideration for others and can teach us how to make **connections** later on in other **contexts**.

Use this table to reflect on your own learning in this chapter					
Questions we asked	Answers we found	Any further questions now?			
Factual: What personality traits do you possess? How can others learn about your personality?					
Conceptual: What is friendship?					
Debatable: Do you know who your real friends are? Can very different people be friends?					
Approaches to learning you used in this chapter	Description – what new skills did you learn?	How well did you master the skills?			
		Novice	Learner	Practitioner	Expert
Communication skills					
Collaboration skills					
Organization skills					
Affective skills					
Reflection skills					
Information literacy skills					
Media literacy skills					
Critical-thinking skills					
Creative-thinking skills					
Learner profile attribute(s)	Reflect on the importance of being principled for your learning in this chapter.				
Principled					

2 Where would we be without family?

○ Our personal and extended family **connections** give **meaning** and a sense of **purpose** to our unique **identities** and **relationships**.

CONSIDER THESE QUESTIONS:

Factual: What is a family? Who is in your family? How far back can you trace your family history? Is there anything funny about your family?

Conceptual: What makes a family?

Debatable: How do cultural factors help to define you as a member of a family, community and culture? Why is family important?

Now **share and compare** your thoughts and ideas with your partner, or with the whole class.

■ What does your family tree look like?

○ IN THIS CHAPTER WE WILL ...

■ **Find out about** families, past, present and future.
■ **Explore** what being part of a family means.
■ **Take action** to raise awareness on how we can help support local and global organizations who work with the elderly living in retirement homes and nursing homes.

'We are inevitably our brother's keeper because we are our brother's brother. What affects one directly affects us all indirectly.' – *Dr Martin Luther King, Jr*

■ These Approaches to Learning (ATL) skills will be useful …

- Communication skills
- Reflection skills
- Information literacy skills
- Critical-thinking skills
- Creative-thinking skills
- Transfer skills

● We will reflect on this learner profile attribute …

- **Open-minded** – we appreciate our own culture and that of others and listen to other points of view.

THINK–PAIR–SHARE

On your own, answer the questions about family below. Write down one or two key words in answer to each question. You can write the words in your own language to help you. Talk to your partner and share answers.

- **What does family mean to you?**
- **How would you explain 'family' to someone who did not understand?**
- **Are there different types of families?**
- **What are they?**

Carry out some research about families. Using a search engine, type the word family and note down ideas about and linked to families. Add this information to the ideas you shared with your partner.

◆ Assessment opportunities in this chapter:

- ◆ **Criterion A**: Listening
- ◆ **Criterion B**: Reading
- ◆ **Criterion C**: Speaking
- ◆ **Criterion D**: Writing

KEY WORDS

adolescence	family unit
adopt	nuclear family
bring up	relatives
extended family	siblings
family member	

What is a family?

Family! You can't live with them, but you can't live without them, right? But what is a family? It is true that to define (or to explain) what a family is might not be easy. Our own understanding of family might not fit what we see in our communities. Just look around you. Families are changing and there might be a 'new' definition for family.

Each family is different. They are made up of different people, with different needs, ideas and ways of behaving. It makes families unique, and it can also mean that getting on well with each other can sometimes be a challenge. How often have you been tempted to swap your brother or sister for somebody else?

Society starts with family. We are born into families, and they are where we are looked after and where we learn the skills we need to survive. Families exist in every animal species. Families have the greatest potential to help individuals to grow and be happy, but they can also present difficulties and affect who we become.

In this chapter, we will focus on the purpose of a family, and how belonging to a family unit helps us to share, communicate and understand the needs of others.

ⓘ Did you know that until the late seventeenth century, 'family' included not only relatives but also the servants of a household. In fact, the word comes from the Latin *famulus*, meaning 'a servant'. Visit the website below to find more facts about family that may surprise you.

www.express.co.uk/life-style/top10facts/399602/Top-10-facts-about-families

ACTIVITY: Find the mistakes!

■ ATL

Reflection skills: Focus on the process of creating by imitating the work of others

Communication skills: Write for different purposes

Task 1

Choose the correct possessive adjective.

her	his	my	our	their	your

1 My name is Jacopo. _____ mother is Jana and _____ father is Pietro. I'm _____ son.
2 My name is Sahara. _____ parents are Rosa and Miguel. I'm _____ daughter.
3 My name is Georg. I have a new sister. _____ name is Barbara. My mother is Lisa and my father is Giovanni. _____ last name is Bertolli.

Task 2

On your own, find the mistakes in this text. Compare your answers with a partner.

```
I have a siter. She is yonger than me. So
I am the older. We were borned in London.
We have been livethere until the we start
school. Then my sister and I move to
London to go to school.

These is or family home. I live hear with
my parent and my pet dog Monty. We have
large garden with trees. I like help mum
in the garden.

My dad is a busness man and my mum is a
housewive. I like living in London but
I mis Athens and my family, especialy my
grandmother.
```

Task 3

Now it's your turn. Write 100-words about your family.

◆ Assessment opportunities

In this activity you have practised skills that are assessed using Criterion B: Reading and Criterion D: Writing.

Writing a paragraph

A **paragraph** is a group of sentences. Paragraphs make your writing clear. Make sure it is easy to see when a new paragraph begins. Leave a little gap or indentation between the margin and the first word. When you make a new point start a new paragraph.

Descriptive paragraphs help us to visualize what a person, a place, a thing or an idea looks, feels, smells and/or tastes like. An adjective is a word that gives more details about a noun. Adjectives are very important for descriptive writing. Adjectives add detail and make our writing interesting.

ACTIVITY: Using vocabulary

■ ATL

Reflection skills: Develop new skills, techniques and strategies for effective learning

Read the definition and guess the family word.

1 **Your sister's daughter** _ _ _ _ _
2 **Your sister's son** _ _ _ _ _ _
3 **Your grandmother's mother**
   _ _ _ _ _ - _ _ _ _ _ _ _ _ _ _
4 **Your brothers and sisters** _ _ _ _ _ _ _ _
5 **Your wife's brother** _ _ _ _ _ _ _ - _ _ - _ _ _
6 **The son of your mother's new husband**
   _ _ _ _ _ _ _ _ _ _

◆ Assessment opportunities

In this activity you have practised skills that are assessed using Criterion D: Writing.

ⓘ A **noun** is a word that identifies a person, place or thing, or names one of them. If the word names a thing, it is called a proper noun.

ACTIVITY: Gap-fill – Present simple tense

■ ATL

Reflection skills: Develop new skills, techniques and strategies for effective learning

Use the verbs from the box below to complete the text that follows.

are	prepare	gets	have
is	live	makes	meet
see	stay	communicate	

We _____ a lot of relatives. My aunt and two uncles _____ in a small town about 50 kilometres from my hometown. Their children, my cousins, are about my age, and we _____ often. Every year the whole family _____ together for Christmas. We _____ a huge Christmas dinner, and there _____ a lot of presents for everyone. My grandparents _____ with us during the holiday. It _____ them very happy to _____ all the extended family together. Family _____ very important in our culture and we always _____ for important celebrations.

◆ Assessment opportunities

In this activity you have practised skills that are assessed using Criterion D: Writing.

What makes a family?

In recent times, there have been important changes in family structure. Divorce rates are on the increase, resulting in more single-parent households, remarriages, blended and extended families. There has also been a rise in unmarried and same-sex couples raising children in many countries in the West.

Most of the time when a person thinks of the definition of a family, the image of a mother, father and children is what comes into the mind. This is what we call a nuclear family, which is parents, and one or more children.

However, there are more definitions that can be used to define a family such as a single-parent family, which is one parent and a child or children. 'Extended family' includes grandparents, uncles, aunts and cousins. In many countries a nuclear family will live under the same roof as an extended family. Would you like to live in a house full of relatives?

ACTIVITY: What makes a family?

■ ATL

Critical-thinking skills: Formulate factual, topical, conceptual and debatable questions

Collaboration skills: Listen actively to other perspectives and ideas

Communication skills: Take effective notes in class

Task 1

In pairs, look at the images above and make notes on what you see. **Discuss** the following:
- **What message do you get about 'family' from each photograph?**
- **What kind of families do you see?**

- **Do the pictures change the way you think about family? Why? Why not?**
- **Looking at the images, what do you think makes a family?**

Task 2

Share your ideas with your classmates. **Create** a class word web with words and phrases to **summarize** your ideas on what makes a family.

◆ Assessment opportunities

In this activity you have practised skills that are assessed using Criterion C: Speaking.

ACTIVITY: Role play
– new neighbour

In the USA, it is a custom to greet new neighbours by knocking on their door, welcoming them, introducing yourself and sometimes taking something you have baked. It is a nice gesture to make a great first impression and possibly make some new friends.

In pairs, take turns at being the new family in the neighbourhood and the neighbours who greet the new family.

Neighbour greeting new family:
- **Knock on the door of the new neighbour and introduce yourself.**
- **Explain how long you have lived there and who else lives with you.**
- **Ask your neighbour any appropriate questions about themselves and their family.**

New neighbour:
- **Ask about the area and facilities such as public transport and shops.**
- **Invite the neighbour in to meet your family.**

◆ Assessment opportunities

In this activity you have practised skills that are assessed using Criterion C: Speaking.

ℹ A **ritual** is a ceremony or action performed in a customary way. Many of us of have rituals we share with friends or family. For example, your family might have a Sunday afternoon ritual of watching a movie together or playing some board games.

■ Elephant family

ACTIVITY: The family structure of elephants

Follow the link below to watch the short clip of biologist Caitlin O'Connell-Rodwell talk about the family structure of elephants.

As you listen:
- **Make some notes about the similarities between human and elephant families.**
- **Consider some of the challenges elephant families face.**
- **Identify the structures established in an elephant family.**
- **Identify the IB learner profile used for the male elephants.**

http://ed.ted.com/lessons/the-family-structure-of-elephants-caitlin-o-connell-rodwell

In pairs, **discuss** and **evaluate** the following:
- **Caitlin's idea that elephant families are like human families – do you agree with her?**
- **The importance of rituals in communities.**

◆ Assessment opportunities

In this activity you have practised skills that are assessed using Criterion A: Listening.

ACTIVITY: Who is your family?

Read the following text and answer the questions.

- **Identify what a 'nuclear family' is.**
- **Where are 'nuclear families' popular?**
- **What different types of families are there nowadays?**
- **How has marriage and bringing up children changed since 1971?**
- **Do you agree or disagree with the ideas in the text?**
- **How will families change in the future?**
- **Find a word in the text that is similar to the words below:**
  - ○ beginning
  - ○ children
  - ○ decreasing
  - ○ difficult
  - ○ emphasizes
  - ○ help with
  - ○ provider
  - ○ relative.

■ Home is where the heart is

The *nuclear family* is the traditional family structure in the West. This term, originating in the 1950s, describes families consisting of a father, a mother, and their offspring. Under this traditional structure, the family is seen as the basic unit in society; the father functions as the breadwinner and the mother as the homemaker. It was a popular model in the 1960s too.

Nowadays, alternative family types are becoming more common, such as single-parent families and families headed by same-sex parents. Extended families where families live with their kin, which may include several generations are becoming less common in the West, where it is not unusual to place grandparents in retirement homes.

A Social Trends survey in 2009 reported radical changes in bringing up children and marriage practices in the United Kingdom. Figures showed that while 30 per cent of women under 30 had given birth by the age of 25, only 24 per cent had married. This marked the first time that childbirth had become the first important step in adult life, ahead of marriage. In 1971 in the UK, three-quarters of women were married by the age of 25 and half were mothers.

Judging by the high rates of divorce and the increasing number of children born out of marriage, it would seem that the family as an institution is in decline. American sociologist Stephanie Coontz believes so too, but for different reasons. Coontz highlights that marriages are no longer arranged for political or economic reasons, and children are no longer required to contribute to the family income. Marriages nowadays are founded on love.

Nowadays, there are different types of nuclear families, for example, one where the man stays at home and looks after the children and the woman goes to work, or the most common one today where both adults go out to work and if they have children they are looked after by someone else. Nearly 60 per cent of women with children under the age of six were in jobs during the last 20 years.

Family units have changed and are still changing. It is becoming more complex. These changes will shape the societies we live in. Families will continue to change, adapt and reflect the new things that are happening in our world. Many people believe that despite the changes, there will always be families. The question is, what kind of families? What do you think the family of the future will look like?

LISTEN–THINK–SHARE

ATL

Communication skills: Preview and skim texts to build understanding

Listen to the song 'That's what I call home' by Blake Shelton, who is an American country singer, by going to YouTube and searching for That's what I call home.

Task 1

In pairs, complete the lyrics by filling in the gaps with words from the box.

built	changed	city	door	feel
good	grew up	handshake	home	house
life	love	paved	raised	road
wood	world			

Follow the link below to check your answers.

http://genius.com/Blake-shelton-thats-what-i-call-home-lyrics

Task 2

In pairs, **discuss** the following questions and support your answers with examples from the song.

1 How does the man in the song feel about his home?
2 How does he describe his home?
3 How does he describe his parents?
4 Where did the man in the song grow up?
5 **Summarize** the main idea of the song in one sentence.
6 How do you feel about your home?
7 How is your home different from your grandparents' home when they were growing up?

There's a _____ that's a little run down
This _____ ain't never found
It's miles and miles from a _____ road
That's where we _____ ____
Seven children _____ on love
When _____ gets hard that's where we go
Daddy don't know a stranger
A _____ and he's your friend
Oh, and mama she's an angel
She'll hold you tight till the heartache ends
Just a place made of nails and _____
But it's the _____ that makes you feel so

_____
That's what I call, that's what I call _____
Daddy _____ it with his own two hands
Overlooking his grandpa's land
Now through the years a lot has _____
But drivin' up this gravel _____
I get that feelin' in my soul
I thank God some things still remain
[Chorus]
Once I get myself
Through that old screen _____
The _____ can't touch me anymore
[Chorus]

◆ Assessment opportunities

In this activity you have practised skills that are assessed using Criterion A: Listening.

ACTIVITY: Spanish family life

Task 1

Use a verb in the present simple or present continuous tense to complete the gaps. Check your answers with a partner. If you are not sure about which tense to use, don't worry – just make a note and check the rules for using each tense.

Can you think of any ways to help you remember when to use each tense?

■ Spanish family life

This is Oscar and his family. They _____ in a detached house in Salamanca. Oscar _____ with his mother, his father, and younger brother Hugo and his younger sisters, Noelia and Sandra. They _____ a big garden with lots of trees. Oscar _____ his mother water and look after the plants.

Today is Sunday, at the moment he _____ lunch with his family on the garden terrace. Sometimes when all the extended family _____ together they _____ a barbecue.

This afternoon, Oscar and Hugo _____ to go to the cinema with their father. Every other Sunday afternoon, Oscar's mother _____ his aunt Merce and they _____ his grandmother who _____ on her own. They _____ her out for chocolate with churros in a nearby cafeteria. Some weekends, his grandma _____ with them, and their cousins _____ in the afternoon. Oscar's two sisters _____ at home to _____ the TV. Some friends _____ to _____ them.

EXTENSION

Bring photos of your families for a class display about 'Our unique families'. Be original and bring a photo that says something special about your family. Write a few sentences about the photo and what it means to you. Use the IB learner profile attributes to talk about your families. Which ones fit your family best?

My Family's Fond of Gadgets

My family's fond of gadgets
and new technology.
My mother likes her radio.
My father likes TV.

My sister likes to dance around
the house with headphones on.
My brother plays on his PC
until the break of dawn.

The baby has a smartphone
and a touchscreen-tablet too.
If we had pets, I'm sure
that even they would have a few.

We chat with instant messaging.
We email and we text.
We're always looking forward
to the gadget we'll get next.

The power went out recently.
That day was like no other.
Our screens went blank and, strange but true,
we talked to one another.

Kenn Nesbitt

Creating a vlog

Video blogging (that is, vlogging) is similar to internet TV. Bloggers can film themselves on video, upload the clip to a host site like YouTube, and then embed a link on their blog to share with the world.

Create a vlog or video that shows how you spend your weekend with your family to share with your classmates. It's easy and fun to do. Just follow these guidelines:

- Choose a name for your vlog.
- Think about the content and prepare what you want to say before you start to film.
- Think about where you are going to film, and customize your vlog design and layout.
- Film your first vlog post – you will need a device to film your vlog. Now that you've got your footage, you'll need video editing software to help you cut, trim and tie it all together.
- Share your vlog with your class when you have finished.

Follow this link to see an example of a family vlog: **www.youtube.com/watch?v=nHcCVtnS2qs**.

ACTIVITY: Is there anything funny or different about your family?

ATL

Creative-thinking: Create original works and ideas; use existing works and ideas in new ways

Read the poem 'My Family's Fond of Gadgets' by Kenn Nesbitt.

Discuss the following questions:

- **Does the poem represent what modern families are like today?**
- **How much time do you spend with your family?**
- **What activities do you do as a family?**

Have a go at creating your own funny family poem. **Identify** five things that are unique to your family.

Assessment opportunities

In this activity you have practised skills that are assessed using Criterion B: Reading and Criterion D: Writing.

How far back can you trace your family history?

■ Making family memories

There are many reasons to know our family history. It provides a living connection to the past and can help us to identify a pattern that we can use to trace and find our origins and roots. Creating a family tree is a fantastic way to start finding out about our family history, which is also known as **genealogy**.

Have you ever heard the saying 'like two peas in a pod'? Well, you might have more in common with your great-grandparents than you think! Discovering who our ancestors are gives families an opportunity to connect by sharing stories and passing them on to younger generations. Through this, we can learn more about our own identities and explore our relationships with others.

In many cultures tracing family roots and sharing information with family members has been the key to preserving family history, one memory at a time. Family elders are not only knowledgeable because of their life experiences, but also because they have significant vivid memories about what happened 40 years ago.

THINK–PAIR–SHARE

■ ATL

Creative-thinking skills: Make unexpected or unusual connections between objects and/or ideas

On your own, answer the following questions:
- **Who is in the old photograph above?**
- **What's happening in the photo?**
- **What old family stories might be connected with the photograph?**

Share your ideas with a partner and write a 100-word paragraph about this photograph.

EXTENSION

Learning about your family history can bring you a wealth of information about the old family photos that are currently a mystery. Look through your own family photos. Choose one to share with your class and prepare a two-minute presentation.

◆ Assessment opportunities

In this activity you have practised skills that are assessed using Criterion D: Writing.

When we ask our family members to remember their past it can strengthen family bonds and help us better understand who we are and where we come from.

Do a little detective work and talk to your families. Look at family mementos (objects that are kept to remind us of people). Ask members of your family how they felt at certain points in the past. How do they feel now, looking back? What surprises will you find?

THINK–PAIR–SHARE

Read the quotes about family and check any unfamiliar words. Use an online dictionary and thesaurus. You can also write a definition in your own language.

In pairs, **analyse** the quotes. Think about the following:
- **What do you think each quote means?**
- **Which attitudes are being expressed in these quotes?**
- **Which one do you like the most? Explain why.**
- **What would your family quote be? Have a go at writing one.**

Important families are like potatoes. The best parts are underground. *Francis Bacon*

There is no doubt that it is around the family and the home that all the greatest virtues, the most dominating virtues of humans, are created, strengthened and maintained. *Winston Churchill*

Family faces are magic mirrors looking at people who belong to us, we see the past, present, and future. *Gail Lumet Buckley*

What can you do to promote world peace? Go home and love your family. *Mother Theresa*

I was angry and frustrated until I started my own family and my first child was born. Until then I didn't really appreciate life the way I should have, but fortunately I woke up. *Johnny Depp*

Family means no one gets left behind or forgotten. *David Ogden Stiers*

An ounce of blood is worth more than a pound of friendship. *Spanish proverb*

What greater thing is there for two human souls than to feel that they are joined for life – to be with each other in silent unspeakable memories. *George Eliot*

ACTIVITY: Family history records

Genealogists often use many different types of records to trace their family trees. Look at the jumbled-up words for records below. How many can you unscramble?

Use a word unscrambler tool to check your answer. Go to http://wordunscrambler.me.

enuscs	dlo ertltse	hspraptogho
tarilimy aerpps	teemryce	uhhrcc dcreors
ilfaym beibl	ilwl	iargamre tifiertcace
notw alhl	uaboitry	

◆ Assessment opportunities

In this activity you have practised skills that are assessed using Criterion B: Reading.

ACTIVITY: Your family tree

In pairs, use interrogative words to make a list of questions to interview members of your families. The purpose is to identify as many facts as you can to make your own digital family tree. You can make notes or record your interviews.

To help you begin, go to the Family Echo website: www.familyecho.com.

◆ Assessment opportunities

In this activity you have practised skills that are assessed using Criterion D: Writing.

ℹ An **interrogative word** or question word is a word used to ask a question, such as *what, when, where, who, whom, why* and *how, how much, how many* and *how far*. They are sometimes called wh- words, because in English most of them start with wh- .

▼ Links to: History

What have you learnt about the origin and purpose of sources like oral history? How reliable are these sources to an historian?

Genealogy involves a lot of research. Time is spent tracking down birth and marriage certificates and other official documents that contain important facts about our ancestors.

Oral history is the systematic collection of living people's testimony about their own experiences. Oral history is not folklore, gossip or rumour, but is a person or group's recollection of certain events that have taken place during their lifetime. Interviewing people is a great way of collecting and recording oral history, and can be done by asking suitable questions. Oral history relies on human memory and the spoken word. The means of collection can vary from taking notes by hand to elaborate electronic aural and video recordings.

It's fascinating Grandad, but... One in three children admit they don't want to hear their relatives talk about the old days

One in three children say they don't want to listen to their grandparents because they find them 'boring', according to new research.

These stories from the days of our grandparents are in danger of being lost with 42 per cent of parents saying their children do not listen to such conversations. It is not only personal memories, but forgotten skills our relatives once mastered, like thatching, which is the word for putting a special hay roof on a house, that could be forgotten for ever too.

The research found only 18 per cent of those under 19 regularly sit down with their elders and listen to stories about the 'old days'. And just 19 per cent of parents bother to share significant stories to their kids from previous generations.

Our older relatives will always have captivating stories to tell, having lived through events such as world wars. Comfortingly though, 68 per cent of parents recognize the importance of sharing family histories with the younger generation.

Children won't understand nor appreciate the contributions past generations made, the research by self-publishing company Blurb suggested.

Family expert Liz Frazer said: 'With the likes of computer games, mobile phones and TV around, our children's attention can so easily be distracted. It's really important that as parents we make time to properly engage with them about our family stories and history.'

'To get kids interested about what Grandad did in the "old days" the trick is to turn these family narratives into fascinating stories' Liz added: 'It's also important to provide our children with the knowledge of who we are, where we came from and what our ancestors did. This way we can help instill a sense of identity and pride, which we hope will then aid in future development.'

Adapted from: http://www.dailymail.co.uk/news/article-2133724/Thats-fascinating-Grandad--One-children-admit-dont-want-hear-relatives-talk-old-days.html

---

READ–THINK–DISCUSS

 ATL

Communication skills: Paraphrase accurately and concisely

First reading: Take five minutes to quickly read the text above and note down three interesting facts that the writer mentions about 'listening to stories from our elders'.

Second reading: Take ten minutes to read the text again and identify the main ideas in each paragraph.

In pairs, **discuss** the following:
- **What type of text is it?**
- **Where would you see a text like this?**
- **What is the purpose of the text?**
- **Has this happened to you?**
- **What is your experience?**
- **Do you agree with the writer? Why? Why not?**

Summarize, using your own words, what the text is about.

◆ Assessment opportunities

In this activity you have practised skills that are assessed using Criterion B: Reading.

ACTIVITY: 'A Family Supper'

ATL

Communication skills: Structure information in summaries, essays and reports; use intercultural understanding to interpret communication

Read this adapted extract from the short story 'A Family Supper' by Kazuo Ishiguro.

My|father|was|aformidablelookingman.Andhewasverytraditio nalandoldfashioned.Hedidn'tliketheideasofyoungpeople.Hisscar yappearancemadepeoplefeelnervousabouttalkingtohim.Icouldno tspeakinarelaxedwaywhenhewasnear.Irememberwhenhehitme manytimeswhenIwasyoungbecauseItalkedtoomuch.Aswedrovef romtheairport,therewerelongpausesinourconversation. Afterwehadn'tspokenformanyminutes,Italkedtomydadabouthis business.'Iamsorryitfailed,'Isaid. Myfathersaidhedidn'twanttostartanewbusiness.'WhenIwasyoun g,weonlydidbusinesswithotherJapanesepeople.Iunderstoodthem. NowwehavetodobusinesswithforeignersandIdon'tunderstandthe irwaysofdoingthings.Watanabedidn'teither.' Whenwegothome,wesatinthe**tearoom**.Icouldseeintothegarden.I twasgettingdarkandtherewere**longshadows**. 'I'mgladyouhavecomebacktoJapan,'myfathersaid.'Ihopeyouwillst ayforalongtime.' 'Iamnotsureaboutmyplans,'Ireplied. Myfathersaidhewantedtoforgetaboutourpastdisagreements.Hesa idmymotherhadwantedtoforgetthemtoo.'Idon'tbelieveyouwerebei ngevil(bad).Youwereinfluencedbyothers,'hecontinuedIdidn'twan ttotalkaboutwhathadhappenedsoIsaidweshouldforgetthepast,lik emyfatherhadsuggested.

Draw lines to show where there should be spaces between the words. The first three have been done for you.

In pairs, **discuss** and **evaluate** what kind of man the father is. Which adjectives are used to describe him?

Now it's your turn. Write a 100-word paragraph about a special family meal.

Assessment opportunities

In this activity you have practised skills that are assessed using Criterion B: Reading and Criterion D: Writing.

ACTIVITY: Family values

■ ATL

Transfer skills: Combine knowledge, understanding and skills to create products or solutions

Discuss the following:
- **What are the family values in your country?**
- **What other factors influence family values?**
- **How does the internet influence values today?**

Follow the link below to find out what a coat of arms is.

https://simple.wikipedia.org/wiki/Coat_of_arms

Create a coat of arms for your family that show your family values. Present your family coat of arms to your class. **Explain** each element and why it is important to you.

◆ Assessment opportunities

In this activity you have practised skills that are assessed using Criterion C: Speaking.

ACTIVITY: Describing a photograph

■ ATL

Communication skills: Use a variety of speaking techniques to communicate with a variety of audiences

Task 1

How can you describe and talk about an ordinary picture in an interesting way?

Follow the link below and listen to someone describe a photograph.

As you listen, make notes on:
- **the language used to talk about the photograph**
- **any detail the speaker gives about the photograph.**

http://esol.britishcouncil.org/content/learners/skills/speaking/describing-picture-family-scene

Task 2

Match the phrases below with the numbers in the picture:
- **on the right-hand side**
- **on the left-hand side**
- **at the bottom**
- **at the top**
- **in the background**
- **on the left**
- **on the right**
- **in the foreground**
- **in the middle**
- **in the bottom right-hand corner**
- **in the bottom left-hand corner.**

Hint

For extra practice go back to the link and do the extra exercises.

Task 3

Now it is your turn. In groups of three, take turns to **describe** one of the images below. Give each other feedback and time yourself. Try to speak for two to three minutes.

If you can, why don't you record your description? Reflect on your description. Is there anything you can do to improve it? Set yourself some targets to help you improve.

■ Picture A

■ Picture B

■ Picture C

◆ Assessment opportunities

In this activity you have practised skills that are assessed using Criterion A: Listening and Criterion D: Speaking.

▮ Take action: Help the elderly

! There are elderly people in retirement and nursing homes who do not have any family. Through your school, contact a local retirement home and volunteer to teach the elderly how to develop basic computer skills or host a special event during the holiday as part of your Service in Action programs.

! Think about:

◆ Who will attend your event? Do they have any specific needs?

◆ Where would you hold the event?

◆ What kind of support might you need?

▼ Links to: Individuals and societies

Take a look at photos of families from the era or region that you are studying. What are the factors that influence the makeup of families at different times in history? How do families change over time? Why do they change? What similarities are there?

SOME SUMMATIVE TASKS TO TRY

Use these tasks to apply and extend your learning in this chapter. These tasks are designed so that you can evaluate your learning in the Language acquisition criteria.

THIS TASK CAN BE USED TO EVALUATE YOUR LEARNING IN CRITERION D TO CAPABLE LEVEL

Task 1: Writing

- Read the writing prompts.
- Choose **one** of the prompts.
- Write a personal response with a minimum of 200–250 words.
- Do not use translating devices or dictionaries for this task.
- You will have 60 minutes to complete this task.

The most interesting thing about my family …

A typical weekend with family starts with …

My parents have always raised me to believe …

The smell of my mum's cooking reminds me of …

THIS TASK CAN BE USED TO EVALUATE YOUR LEARNING IN CRITERION C TO CAPABLE LEVEL

Task 2: Interactive oral

Choose one of the prompts from Task 1 and use it as a starting point for an discussion about your family.

If you get stuck, you can use some of the prompts below to help you.

You are expected to speak for 3–4 minutes.

- How big is your family?
- Do you live with your parents?
- Do you live with your grandparents?
- Are you the eldest or the youngest among your brothers and sisters?
- What is the best number of children to have?
- Should people adopt children from other countries?
- How did you get your name?
- Were you named after any member of your family?
- How do you get along with your parents?
- How do you get along with your brothers or sisters?
- How do you get along with your grandparents?
- How often do you visit your grandparents?
- Does your father work?
- Does your mother work?
- Who is the breadwinner in your family?
- Who does the housework in your family?
- Do you help your parents with the housework?
- Should children help with the housework?
- Are your parents strict?
- How many aunts and uncles do you have?
- Do you often meet your aunts and uncles? When?
- How many cousins do you have?
- Do you often meet your cousins? When?
- How important is family in your country?
- Describe a typical family unit in your country. Has it changed over the years?

**THIS TASK CAN BE USED TO EVALUATE YOUR
LEARNING IN CRITERION B AT CAPABLE LEVEL**

Task 3: 'Your Family: Past, Present, and Future' by Tim Urban

Go to **http://waitbutwhy.com/2014/01/your-family-past-present-and-future.html** and read the multimodal text.

- Use your own words as much as possible.
- You cannot use dictionaries for this task.
- You have 60 minutes to complete this task.

1   What did Timothy use his visit for?   (strand i)
2   What does the writer say most people do
    not do?   (strand i)
3   Which word or phrase in the second
    paragraph of the article suggests that many
    people are selfish?   (strand ii)
4   Why has this text been written? What are
    some of the language features that make
    you think this?   (strand ii)
5   a   Find a word in the text that
        means 'act'.   (strand ii)
    b   What effect does the writer achieve by
        using this verb?   (strand ii)
6   Find a word in the article that
    means 'poor'.   (strand ii)
7   Find a word in the article that means
    'absorbed'.   (strand ii)
8   After reading the article do you think that
    more should be done to find out about family
    roots? **Justify** your response with information
    from the text.   (strand iii)
9   Using information provided in the article,
    if you wanted to find out more about your family,
    what could you do?   (strand iii)
10 How successful was the writer in achieving
    his purpose?   (strand i)

11 The family was made unwelcome and treated
    badly by their neighbours. Is this statement
    true or false? Support your answer with evidence
    from the text.   (strand i)
12 Why does the writer say 'thankfully' his
    great-grandmother died before finding out the
    terrible news? Support your answer with evidence
    from the text.   (strand iii)
13 How do the images used in the article help
    to convey the writer's message?   (strand iii)

Task 4: 'The Next America: Modern Family'

- Watch and listen to the video clip.
- Answer the questions below.
- Use your own words as much as possible.
- You cannot use dictionaries in this task.
- You have 60 minutes to complete this task.
- The video clip can be found at:
  www.youtube.com/watch?v=8OQCxgNjbq8.

1 'Marriage is the first step towards starting family.' Support or
  oppose this statement, using examples from the text.   (strand i)

2 **Summarize** in your own words how weddings today
  look different.   (strand i)

3 How would you describe how people feel about marriage in
  the twenty-first century? **Justify** your answer with details
  from the text.   (strand i)

4 What things could people from all cultures learn from
  this text?   (strand i)

5 What type of text is 'The Next America: Modern Family'?   (strand ii)

6 Who is the intended audience? Why do you think so?   (strand ii)

7 What effect does the background music together with the
  visual information create? Support your ideas with examples. (strand ii)

8 The creator purposefully uses scenes from modern times,
  history, dancing and graphs in the video. Why do you think
  he did this? What is the setting of the text?   (strand ii)

9 Can you think of any other cultures where relationships,
  family and marriage are used to talk about communities?
  How are they similar to 'The Next America: Modern Family'?
  How are they different?   (strand iii)

10 Would you recommend this video clip to someone else?
  Why? Why not?   (strand iii)

Reflection

In this chapter we have explored how families help us to understand our place in groups, and **connect** to our communities and the world. We have covered aspects ranging from why we should find out about our ancestors and the **purpose** the family has in shaping our **identities and relationships** with others. In addition we have considered how important the family unit is as a basis for our society.

Use this table to reflect on your own learning in this chapter					
Questions we asked	Answers we found	Any further questions now?			
Factual: What is a family? Who is in your family? How far back can you trace your family history? Is there anything funny about your family?					
Conceptual: What makes a family?					
Debatable: How do cultural factors help to define you as a member of a family, community and culture? Why is family important?					
Approaches to learning you used in this chapter:	Description – what new skills did you learn?	How well did you master the skills?			
		Novice	Learner	Practitioner	Expert
Communication skills					
Reflection skills					
Information literacy skills					
Critical-thinking skills					
Creative-thinking skills					
Transfer skills					
Learner profile attribute(s)	Reflect on the importance of being open-minded for your learning in this chapter.				
Open-minded					

③ Eat to live, or live to eat?

○ **Choices** we make about what we eat are influenced by our **culture** and the **context** in which we live, and might send **messages** about **who we are**.

■ Where does the food we eat come from?

CONSIDER THESE QUESTIONS:

Factual: Where does our food come from? What effect does the food we eat have on our health?

Conceptual: What does the food we eat tell us about who we are? How does food help shape who we are and how we live? How can we ensure that choices we make about food don't have harmful consequences?

Debatable: Can we feed the world? Do we waste too much food?

Now **share and compare** your thoughts and ideas with your partner, or with the whole class.

○ IN THIS CHAPTER WE WILL ...

■ **Find out** where our food comes from and how it is produced.
■ **Explore** how food is eaten and enjoyed around the world.
■ **Take action** to raise awareness about how we can take small steps to help tackle world hunger.

◆ Assessment opportunities in this chapter:

◆ **Criterion A**: Listening
◆ **Criterion B**: Reading
◆ **Criterion C**: Speaking
◆ **Criterion D**: Writing

KEY WORDS

arable
diet
farming
nutritional
pastoral
ritual

■ These Approaches to Learning (ATL) skills will be useful:

- Communication skills
- Collaboration skills
- Information literacy skills

- Affective skills
- Critical-thinking skills
- Creative-thinking skills

● We will reflect on this learner profile attribute …

● **Balanced** – the well-being of both our brains and our bodies depends on making balanced choices.

WATCH–THINK–SHARE

What's in your lunchbox? How might your lunchbox be different from that of a student in France? Follow the links below and watch the short clips on lunchboxes and read the articles.

Identify some of the things you see and consider the importance of the move to improve school lunches.

Share your ideas with a partner.

www.dailymail.co.uk/femail/food/article-2957301/What-school-lunches-look-like-world.html

http://neverseconds.blogspot.co.uk/

Have a go at making your own healthy lunchbox.

How does food help shape who we are and how we live?

FOOD, GLORIOUS FOOD!

We all love to eat, but how many of us stop to think about what we are putting into our bodies? We are spoilt for choice when it comes to food. The shelves in our supermarkets are full to bursting with produce from every corner of the world. But perhaps we need to be a bit more aware of where our food comes from and what we are eating.

Food is not only important for our survival, but it is also closely linked to who we are. What we eat and how we eat often varies depending on where we live and the culture we belong to. Food plays an important role in helping us to preserve our traditions and has the power to bring us closer together. Trying new foods and sharing our own with others is not only satisfying but can also be a great way of learning about other people and cultures.

Today, we are consuming more food than ever before, but sadly with more food comes more waste. Although many of us rarely need to worry about where our next meal is coming from, there are some people around the world who do not have access to the same basic resources we have, let alone some of the more luxurious items that can be found sitting in our kitchen cupboards.

In this chapter we will focus on our complex relationship with food and how we can work together to try and ensure that in the future there will be enough food available to feed the world.

■ Food around the world

■ A-gei, a popular Taiwanese snack, are pouches of fried tofu filled with noodles and served in broth

■ Tom yum gai, Thai chicken soup

■ Italian spaghetti with clams and basil

■ Chicken tikka masala, an Indian dish first created in the UK!

ACTIVITY: Around the world in 80 diets

■ ATL

Information literacy skills: Access information to be informed and inform others

Task 1

In pairs, visit the links below and explore the projects which highlight the different diets around the world. Find out about the food people in different parts of the world like to eat.

Discuss:

● **What ingredients are available to different cultural groups?**
● **How do these ingredients impact on their diets?**
● **What's your point of view on people's preferences?**

Summarize the main points and share with your classmates.

http://content.time.com/time/
photogallery/0,29307,2037749_2219823,00.html

www.theguardian.com/lifeandstyle/gallery/2013/
may/06/hungry-planet-what-world-eats

Task 2

In groups, develop a recipe that is representative of one of the cultures in your group. Present your recipe to the class, describing the ingredients in your recipe and when you would prepare and/or eat this food.

◆ Assessment opportunities

In this activity you have practised skills that are assessed using Criterion B: Reading and Criterion C: Speaking.

How can we ensure that choices we make about food don't have harmful consequences?

WHERE DOES OUR FOOD COME FROM?

The food that finds its way into our kitchens and eventually to our stomachs, comes from many different sources, both local and global. As a result it's easy to lose track of what we're really eating and where it has come from.

In the past, many people grew their own food, but things have changed considerably over time. Today, most of the food we eat comes from farms from across the world. However, by the time some of these foods arrive in our supermarkets, they have become so processed that they bear hardly any resemblance to the products produced by the farmers. Think, for example, how similar your breakfast cornflakes are to an actual ear of corn. Not very, you'll find!

Most farms fall into one of two categories: arable and pastoral. Arable farms concentrate on crops such as oats or wheat, while pastoral farms concentrate on animals. From this latter group we get our meat and dairy products.

Although being able to obtain food from all over the world has its advantages, (how else could we eat delicious exotic fruits all year round?), many people argue that relying too heavily on globally produced foods could have negative long-term consequences.

ⓘ **Locally produced goods** are products grown, sold and usually consumed in the same region.

Globally produced goods are products that are produced, grown and sold in different parts of the world. They may travel hundreds of miles from where they were grown to where they are sold.

ACTIVITY: Where does my food come from?

■ ATL

Information literacy skills: Collect, record and verify data

Task 1

Take a look at the example package label. Where does the product come from?

Task 2

Copy and complete the table below to make a list of all the foods you have eaten since this morning. Do you know where the food on your list comes from or how it was produced?

Use a search engine and type in each product to find the answer to these questions. You can also go to a supermarket website and look at the packaging information for the product.

Food	Where does it come from? (Place of origin)	How was it produced?

What surprised you most about what you found out through your research?

◆ Assessment opportunities

In this activity you have practised skills that are assessed using Criterion B: Reading.

WATCH–THINK–SHARE

■ ATL

Critical-thinking skills: Evaluate evidence and arguments

Should all our food be produced locally?

Watch this short clip of 11-year-old Birke Baehr talking about what he believes is wrong with our food system: www.ted.com/talks/birke_baehr_what_s_wrong_with_our_food_system?language=en.

As you listen:

- **Make some notes about what Birke says is wrong with the way our food is produced.**
- **Consider some of the things Birke suggests as alternatives.**
- **Identify the advantages of producing food locally.**

In pairs, **discuss** and **evaluate** the following:

- **Birke's proposals – do you agree with him?**
- **The possible disadvantages of producing food locally.**

◆ Assessment opportunities

In this activity you have practised skills that are assessed using Criterion A: Listening.

EXTENSION

1 Find out about the following: factory farming; free range; organic farming. Make notes on all the terms. **Evaluate** what you learn and decide what you think is the best method.

2 **Explore** to what extent your local supermarkets support local farmers. Find out where your parents do their weekly grocery shop. Do they only shop at large supermarkets or do they make use of the independent retailers in your local area?

Visit the website of a major supermarket you have been to. Search for local produce.

Find out:
- how committed they are to providing their customers with local produce
- how much of their stock is globally produced
- how you can support local food production.

Making notes

Taking good notes helps you focus on and organize the information you need to study and learn. The most important thing about note taking is that you need to do more than simply listen and write. What strategies do you use to take notes? Do you have a special way to make notes?

To take good notes you need to listen, think, respond, question, summarize, organize, label and write.

10 steps on 'How to make notes'

1 Label and date your notes at the beginning of the page.
2 Read or listen to the text carefully and make sure you understand what it is about.
3 Write your notes as neatly as you can.
4 Work out what the important facts are.
5 Select information – you do not want sentences, you want:
   - single words (especially nouns, adjectives, verbs)
   - short phrases
   - use your own words.
6 Relate the material to something in your life by writing an example or a reminder.
7 Use colours to highlight important sections or things you do not understand.
8 Use lines and arrows to show the links between things.
9 Use a system or note-taking guide that works for you.
10 Ask questions when you do not understand something and always re-read your notes.

You can always complete any gaps you have when you go over your notes!

Speech bubble (Anthony Bourdain): I would like to see people more aware of where their food comes from. I would like to see small farmers empowered.

Speech bubble (Joel Salatin): Know your food, know your farmers, and know your kitchen.

■ Anthony Bourdain, Chef

■ Joel Salatin, Farmer

ACTIVITY: Knowing where food comes from

Read the quotes above and answer the questions below.

- **What do you think these quotes mean?**
- **How do these quotes link to what you have learnt so far in this chapter?**
- **Will you think more carefully about where your food comes from? Explain why.**
- **How can you find out about where it comes from and how it is produced?**

■ ATL

Critical thinking: Draw reasonable conclusions and generalizations

◆ Assessment opportunities

In this activity you have practised skills that are assessed using Criterion B: Reading.

THINK–PAIR–SHARE

Discuss these quotes by people involved in the food industry. Where would you see these quotes? How might these quotes influence people's point of view? Do you know any other famous food quotes?

What effect does the food we eat have on our health?

WHAT IS A HEALTHY DIET?

We all have different ideas about what makes a perfect diet. For some, taste is everything, while for others, it's all about making healthy choices. They say variety is the spice of life, and today we have access to more foods than ever before. We have become more experimental in our kitchens and are more willing to try out the vast array of new and exciting ingredients that can be found at our local shops and in our supermarkets.

But what does a healthy diet look like? Most nutritionists agree that a balanced, healthy diet should consist of lots of fruits and vegetables, starchy foods such as potatoes, bread, rice and pasta and plenty of beans, fish, eggs, milk and other dairy products. Meat is important as we need iron, but should be eaten in moderation. Experts also recommend that we think carefully about the amount of sugar and salt we consume, as too much of these can be harmful to our health.

As our lives get busier, it can be harder to ensure that we are eating healthily. While we can celebrate the fact that over the past two decades consumption of fruits and vegetables has improved worldwide, we cannot ignore the worrying statistics which tell us that the amount of unhealthy, processed food we eat is also on the rise.

These days it's all too easy to pick up a convenient supermarket ready meal full of artificial flavourings and preservatives to help us save time or to snack on something unhealthy to keep us going throughout the day. But if we're not careful, we risk developing serious health problems.

Idioms and sayings

There are many, food-inspired **idioms** in the English language including some of the following:

- Variety is the spice of life.
- My body is a temple.
- You are what you eat.

What do you think each one might mean? Do you know of any food idioms from your own culture or country?

■ A balanced diet is a healthy diet

My body is my temple. I exercise a lot and have a very strict diet because I want to live a full, happy and healthy life. I never eat junk food and make sure that I only ever buy organic fruit and vegetables. The thought of all those pesticides makes me feel sick! I prepare all my own meals because it's important for me to know what I'm putting into my body. On an average day I'll start with some healthy granola for breakfast and then have a salad for lunch. In the evening I'll probably have a piece of chicken or some fish with some brown rice or steamed vegetables. I wouldn't touch a supermarket ready meal and just don't understand why so many people eat them!

As a student, I don't have much money and, to be honest, I can't really be bothered with cooking a proper meal from scratch every evening. These days you can pick up almost anything from the shops and if I can cook a curry in my microwave in less than five minutes, why would I want to waste time chopping up meat and veg? It's much cheaper than buying fresh ingredients too. If I'm eating with friends we usually pitch in and order food – nothing special, usually just a pizza or something. I have to confess, I do eat a fair amount of junk like crisps, fizzy drinks, fast food, but hey, you only live once and I'm still young, so why shouldn't I just enjoy it?

■ Gaia, 27

■ Georg, 19

THINK–PAIR–SHARE

■ ATL

Collaboration skills: Listen actively to other perspectives and ideas

Read the statements above and decide who you think has the **most balanced diet**.

Share your ideas with a partner and **discuss** the different lifestyle choices people make.

Most people don't realize just how much damage eating meat and other animal products causes to the environment. I care about the planet, which is why I decided to go vegan two years ago. As a vegan I don't eat any meat, fish, dairy products, eggs or honey. Instead I get all I need from vegetables, grains, fruits, beans and pulses. I'm often asked if I miss any particular foods, and I have to admit, at the beginning, it was hard giving up so much. I used to love cheese but now I just snack on nuts and seeds which are just as tasty. People always imagine that vegans are weak and sickly, but I've never felt healthier.

I have two young children and my husband to cater for and I want to make sure that they're getting all the nutritional goodness they need. I make sure we have a variety of foods and like to think that I'm quite an experimental cook – just the other night I made paella for the first time. The kids loved it! Although I try my best to put a home-cooked meal on the table every night, sometimes I will just stick a ready meal in the oven. Of course I want my kids to be healthy, but I don't think there's any harm in letting them have a nice sweet treat once in a while. A bit of chocolate or a scoop of ice cream always puts a smile on their little faces!

■ Dulce, 22

■ Antonella, 36

Think about the following:

- **Who is the healthiest eater?**
- **Who is the least healthy eater?**
- **Who has the most balanced diet?**
- **Which diet is closest to your own?**
- **What do you think people need to eat in order to have a balanced diet?**

Do you agree with your partner about what we need to eat in order to have a balanced diet?

▼ Links to: Science

Food as fuel

The next time you're about to eat something, check out the nutritional information on the packaging and you'll find that you probably need an encyclopaedia to understand what it all means.

Alongside a list of ingredients, you'll often find details of the energy the food will provide you with and information about what are known as the **food groups**.

These food groups include **carbohydrates**, **fats**, **proteins**, **fibre**, **vitamins** and **minerals**. Each of these food groups affect your body in a different way and in order to have a balanced diet you need to make sure that you get the appropriate quantity of all of these.

To learn how these food groups affect your body see *Sciences for the IB MYP 1*.

THINK–PUZZLE–EXPLORE

Take a look at the nutritional information on packaging. What percentage of your daily requirement of each food group does each item contain? Does this surprise you? Explore your kitchen cupboard and find some foods you enjoy eating. Look at the food labels and evaluate how balanced they are.

EXTENSION: ARE YOU GETTING YOUR FIVE A DAY?

Carry out some research about what five a day refers to.

What did you discover? How can you ensure you're getting your five a day?

What does the food we eat tell us about who we are?

THE HUMBLE SANDWICH

As our lives get busier and busier it can be hard always to eat properly, especially when we're out and about. There are so many options available, but nothing can ever really beat the humble sandwich. Tasty, satisfying and incredibly easy to prepare, our love affair with this timeless classic goes back hundreds of years.

ℹ Did you know that although we're not entirely sure where the idea of the sandwich originated, we *can* trace the word back to John Montagu, the fourth Earl of Sandwich (Kent, England)? The story goes that one day, not wanting to interrupt a game of cards he was playing, he asked his servant to bring him some meat served between two slices of bread. And that's how the sandwich got its name!

Do you ever have sandwiches for lunch? What do you like most about sandwiches? What's your favourite sandwich?

■ Did the Earl of Sandwich really invent this lunchtime favourite?

Writing a set of instructions

Here are some tips to help you write:

- Guidelines on how to prepare food are usually known as **recipes**.
- Use the **present simple tense** to give instructions. Think of some **verbs** you might want to use, for example: *spread, wash, cut, put.*
- Make sure your sentences are **clear** and **simple**. Use **discourse markers** such as: *first, next, now, then, finally.* Can you think of any others?
- Present your guidelines in a logical order. You may want to number them.
- If you want some guidance, try looking up a recipe. There are plenty online or maybe someone at home has recipe book lying around.
- Start by giving your reader a list of what they will need to make the sandwich.

  You will need two slices of bread, some butter and ...

  [Add any other ingredients you want to include to this list.]

  First ...

Why not test out your guidelines by getting a friend or family member to try making your sandwich?

READ–THINK–WRITE

■ ATL

Communication skills: Use appropriate forms of writing for different purposes and audiences

Write a set of **guidelines** for how to make a sandwich of your choice. Think about how sandwiches take on different forms depending on where you are in the world. Your sandwich could be an Italian panini, a Cuban sandwich, a Greek gyros or a Mexican burrito!

◆ Assessment opportunities

In this activity you have practised skills that are assessed using Criterion D: Writing.

How does the food we eat, and the way we eat it, reflect our culture?

■ Eid celebrations in Tajikistan

The food we eat often says a great deal about who we are. Food is so closely linked to our identity, to our culture, to our collective and individual histories. Food can be a reminder of personal experiences; it connects us to our families and can transport us to other worlds simply through our taste buds.

Stepping into any supermarket today we can see just how diverse our tastes have become. We can find food from Italy, China, Mexico, India, the West Indies, Nigeria and Poland to name but a few. Travel and migration have had an incredible impact on the way we think about and prepare food. Our kitchens have become global kitchens and by eating the food of people from other cultures we can begin to gain an understanding and insight into their customs, traditions and values, and most importantly see just how much we all have in common.

A ritual is a ceremony or action performed in a customary way. Many of us of have rituals we share with friends or family. Most cultures have rituals that revolve around food, such as eating roast turkey on Thanksgiving or giving up certain foods during Lent. These actions are often symbolic and carry cultural or religious significance. They allow us to express our beliefs and remind us about where we come from.

■ Thanksgiving, USA

■ Easter in Bosnia and Herzegovia

■ Chinese New Year, China

ACTIVITY: Food rituals

Task 1

Go to the British Library website at: www.bl.uk/learning/citizenship/foodstories/index.html.

Click on the LAUNCH INTERACTIVE button and spend some time exploring all the goodies in the kitchen cupboard.

Then click on the RITUAL AND TRADITION link. We have already come across rituals in Chapter 2.

Click on the bright pink tin and listen to what Shezad has to say about Eid celebrations.

Complete the following tasks.

1 **Identify** some of the foods that Shezad's family would eat on Eid.
2 **What role do you think that food plays in the Eid ritual for Shezad's family?**
3 **Think of all the festivals or events you have celebrated in the past. Did you have any special foods on those occasions? List some of these dishes.**

Task 2

Look at the images on page 60 showing the celebration of different festivals from around the world.

What do they all have in common?

In a table like the one below, write down some adjectives you could use to describe what you see. Try to come up with some really interesting ones!

Eid	Easter	Thanksgiving	Chinese New Year

Choose one of the pictures and write a short paragraph describing what you see.

Think about the following:

- **What colours can you see? Are the foods of different shapes and sizes? What about the amount of food? How is it arranged?**
- **Imagine how the food might taste or smell? What might it feel like when you touch it or put it in your mouth?**
- **Think about the atmosphere. How would you describe it?**

ACTIVITY: Using tenses

The **past simple** and the **past continuous** tenses are very useful when writing to describe. We often use these tenses together. When this happens, the past continuous describes a longer action or situation and the past simple describes the action or events.

Look at this example:

As I was walking to school this morning, I saw a magnificent rainbow in the sky!

   (past continuous)   (past simple)

Remember that irregular verbs are tricky. You might need to check the irregular forms in a dictionary.

Practise using the tenses by copying and completing the sentences below with an appropriate form of the verb in brackets.

1 **You (study) _____ in an international school in Paris when I (meet) _____ you.**
2 **When I (walk) _____ into the classroom the students (sit) _____ at their desks.**
3 **As soon as I (see) _____ the woman about to cross the road, I (shout) _____ to warn her, but it (be) _____ too late! The driver (drive) _____ very fast and he (not, stop) _____.**
4 **When I (receive) _____ the letter, I (study) _____ for my final exams.**

Similes – Writing to describe

Do you want to make your descriptive writing more imaginative? Use a **simile**!

A simile is a way of describing something by comparing it to something else, usually using the word 'like' or 'as'.

Here are some examples:

■ He runs like a cheetah

■ Her lips were as red as rubies

What do you think these similes suggest?

Practise writing some of your own similes using the prompts below:

1   His eyes were …
2   She shouted …
3   The bed is …
4   I felt …
5   The food was …

EXTENSION: EXPLORE FOOD RITUALS FURTHER

Choose a food ritual and carry out some research.

Consider the following questions to help you:
- What is the food ritual?
- Where is it practised and by whom?
- How often does it take place?
- What does it symbolize?
- What does it involve? Which foods are eaten?

Present your findings in a poster, which you can display in your classroom.

ACTIVITY: Food tales

■ ATL

Communication skills: Read critically and for comprehension

Every dish has a story to tell, so it's only natural that most cultures have myths or folktales based on food. These stories can tell us about the origin or cultural significance of a particular food or reveal truths about human behaviour and there is often an important lesson to be learnt.

'Stone soup' is one such folktale that seems to resurface in a number of different cultures, each time with slight variations. This particular version is set in Switzerland. Read the story on page 63 and consider the following questions:

- **Summarize what you think the *moral* or message of the story is.**
- **Is the pebble really magical? What is its actual purpose?**
- **What do you think this story reveals about human behaviour?**

Did you enjoy this story? Do you know any stories about food? In pairs or groups, share your stories and **discuss** and reflect on whether we can learn anything from them.

◆ Assessment opportunities

In this activity you have practised skills that are assessed using Criterion B: Reading.

Stone soup

One morning, an exhausted traveller arrived at a small village in Switzerland. He saw a woman sitting at the door of her cottage. She was busy spinning but stopped to speak to the traveller when he came up to her. He told her the roads were in poor condition and that he was excited about his trip along the banks of the River Rhine. At last he asked her if she had any fire.

'To be sure I have! How else would I cook my dinner?' she replied.

'Oh, then,' said the traveller, 'as your pot is on, you can give me a little warm water.'

'To be sure I can! But what do you want with warm water?'

'If you will lend me a small pot,' said the traveller, 'I'll show you.'

'Well, you shall have a pot. There, now what do you want with it?'

'I want,' said the traveller, 'to make some stone soup!'

'Stone soup!' cried the woman. 'I've never heard of that before. What will you make it out of?'

'I will show you in an instant,' said the man and opened his wallet. From it, he took out a large smooth pebble.

'Here,' he cried, 'is the main ingredient. Now toast me a large slice of bread.'

The stone was dropped into the warm water. The bread was toasted, and put into the pot with it.

'Now,' said the traveller, 'let me have a bit of bacon, a small quantity of *sauerkraut, pepper, and salt, onions, celery and *thyme.'

The woman had a store cupboard and a well-kept vegetable garden, so the ingredients were brought out instantly. The soup began cooking. When the soup was finally ready, the kind woman tasted it and found it was delicious! She was so pleased that she produced all the food she had in her cottage and she, with the traveller, had a hearty meal, with the stone soup as the main dish.

When the traveller got up to leave, he told the good woman, who had carefully washed the stone, that as she has been so kind to him, he would, in return, make her a present of it.

'Where did you get it?' she asked.

'Oh,' he replied, 'I have brought it a considerable way; and it is the type of stone that if it is kept clean, its magic will never run out. With the same ingredients, it will always make as good a soup as that which we have eaten today.'

The woman was very grateful and thanked the traveller as he set out on his journey. She was proud of this discovery and told all of her neighbours.

The recipe became very popular, and after some time the villagers discovered that they could use other pebbles to make the same soup! It became such a popular dish that people from neighbouring areas began to use the recipe. Even to this day, the soup can be found served as a starter in homes across the region.

ℹ **sauerkraut** – a specially prepared cabbage

thyme – a type of herb

Can we feed the world?

HOW CAN WE STOP SO MUCH FOOD FROM GOING TO WASTE?

In a world where we seem to have endless quantities of food available to us and where we have made such profound developments in farming, food production and preservation, it seems utter madness that hunger should be a problem anywhere. But it is.

Why isn't there enough food to feed the world? Hunger is not just about too many people and not enough food. Climate change, the rising cost of food and not having access to resources such as land and equipment are all factors that contribute to people starving all over the world.

Sadly, it will be many years before we can hope to solve the problem of world hunger, but it is important to realize that this is as much a local problem as it is a global one and all of us must do what we can in the fight against it.

Every year a phenomenally large amount of food goes to waste. This is a terrible tragedy as each night millions of people around the world go to sleep hungry. A large proportion of these people are children and teenagers like yourselves. By taking small steps, we can help prevent food being wasted on a daily basis and really make a difference.

ACTIVITY: End world hunger

■ ATL

Communication skills: Make inferences and draw conclusions

Look at the GROW poster on page 65 and consider the following questions:

1 **According to the poster, what can you do to help fight hunger?**
2 **What is the purpose of this multimodal text and who is the target audience?**
3 **How do the visual aspects of the poster link to the written text?**
4 **Evaluate how successful is the poster at achieving its purpose? What features make it effective? List at least five different features.**
5 **How does the poster make you feel? Will it influence the way you think about food?**

◆ Assessment opportunities

In this activity you have practised skills that are assessed using Criterion B: Reading.

GROW

GROW is Oxfam's food justice campaign that aims to raise awareness of the issue of world hunger and how we can do our little bit towards tackling this terrible problem which affects millions of people around the world.

The heading is a **rhetorical question**, which makes the viewer think.

Repetition of grammatical structure: 'buying it, selling it, growing it' – emphasizes how we are all involved with food in some way. It is also catchy and appeals to the viewer.

The **bright colours** and simple pictures engage the audience by making the poster eye-catching and positive.

The text uses **personal pronouns** (we, our, you) and **imperatives** ('look for …', 'find ideas …') to address the audience directly and make us feel involved.

The **image of the globe** flanked by a fork and a knife makes it look like a plate and reinforces the idea that hunger is a global issue that affects us all.

The **logo** and website details show us that this is an Oxfam campaign. It makes it easier for the viewer to find out more.

The simple **layout** (information box) and language make the poster easy to understand and navigate.

Did you know that some 795 million people in the world do not have enough food to lead a healthy active life? That's about one in nine people on Earth.

The World Food Programme is one of many charities dedicated to ending world hunger. Visit their website to find more facts about hunger and what you can do to help: **www.wfp.org/hunger/stats**.

■ World Hunger Map 2019. The World Food Programme is just one of many charities dedicated to ending world hunger

! Take action: How can I make a difference?

! We can all make a small difference by trying to cut down the amount that is wasted on a daily basis.

! Take action …

◆ By making changes in your own household. Keep a diary of all the food that you waste every day. Try to get your parents and brothers and sisters to do the same. Review your findings together as a family at the end of the week. Identify some strategies to stop so much food being thrown away: buy less and cook smaller amounts.

◆ By raising awareness at your local school. Perhaps you can ask your teachers to talk about this in advisory time or even organize a whole school assembly?

! You can find out more and get tips on how you can stop wasting food at: www.bbc.co.uk/guides/zpcyvcw.

SOME SUMMATIVE TASKS TO TRY

Use these tasks to apply and extend your learning in this chapter. These tasks are designed so that you can evaluate your learning in the Language acquisition criteria.

THIS TASK CAN BE USED TO EVALUATE YOUR LEARNING IN CRITERION D TO CAPABLE LEVEL

Task 1: Writing to describe

■ Do not use translating devices or dictionaries for this task.
■ You will have 60 minutes to complete this task.

Look back at the images and captions on page 60. Do you celebrate any of these festivals? Think back to a time when you celebrated a festival or attended an exciting event where food played an important part.

Write a description of the event focusing in particular on the food. You should aim to write 200–250 words.

■ Think carefully about your choice of language (adjectives, verbs, adverbs).
■ Include similes if you can.
■ Think carefully about the senses – what can you see, smell, hear, touch or taste?

Task 2: Why the sky is far away

- Read the folktale from Nigeria on the opposite page and answer the questions that follow.
- Use your own words as much as possible.
- Do not use translating devices or dictionaries for this task.
- You will have 60 minutes to complete this task.

1 Why don't the people on Earth have to work on the land? (strand i)

2 **Identify** some of the flavours described in the text. (strand ii)

3 What makes the sky angry? Choose one of the following:
   a The people eat too much food.
   b The people waste food.
   c The people never thank the sky.
   d The people are lazy. (strand ii)

5 Which word or phrase in the first paragraph of the story suggests that the people are careless about the way they treat the sky? (strand i)

6 How would you describe Osato's personality? **Explain** and support your answer with **two** examples from the text. (strand iii)

7 Look at the image at this weblink **https://tinyurl.com/y82tt2xq**, taken from The Barefoot Book of Earth Tales which contains a version of Osato's story. **Evaluate** how well the illustrator has captured the character of Osato. (strand iii)

8 a **Find** a word in the text that means 'to walk with short steps and a clumsy swaying motion'.
   b What effect does the writer achieve by using this verb? (strand i)

9 The sky eventually forgives the people for their poor behaviour. Is this statement true or false? **Justify** your answer with evidence from the text. (strand i)

10 **Find** a simile in the third paragraph. What does this simile tell us about the people's attitude towards food? (strand ii)

11 What message do you think the writer is trying to convey? **Justify** your answer with evidence from the text. (strand ii)

12 What learner profile attributes do you think Osato and the other people of the village lack? Why do you think this? **Use** evidence from the text to support your answer. (strand iii)

13 **Explain** what would you have done in Osato's shoes? (strand iii)

Many, many years ago, the Earth and sky were so close together that one could reach up and touch it! But the people of the earth didn't just touch it, they ate it too! All the food and nourishment they needed came from the sky and they always had more than enough. No one had to labour in the fields to plough the land, sow seeds or gather crops. Whenever the people felt stirrings of hunger, all they had to do was just reach up and tear off a piece of the sky.

But the people began to abuse the sky's generosity. They grew careless and broke off more than they actually needed to satisfy their hunger. No-one gave a second thought to the food that was plucked from the sky but left uneaten. Why worry when the sky was so big? Surely there would always be enough for everybody? Who cared about a little wasted sky?

The sky cared and grew sad. This sorrow soon turned into resentment and eventually anger. 'I offer myself to them every day,' he said, 'and yet they discard me, half eaten, like garbage!'

'People of Earth!' he bellowed, 'You have treated me disrespectfully and have wasted the gifts I have given you. Take heed of this warning: If you continue to be greedy, I will leave this place and move far away where you cannot reach me.'

The people were frightened and promised to be grateful and to take more care. No-one broke off more than they could eat and for a while, all was well.

But then the day of the people's great festival arrived. This was held every in honour of the chief of the kingdom and the highlight of the day was always the grand feast, prepared specially by the sky.

The tables were piled high with dishes of sky in every flavour imaginable. The sky had provided plentifully, and trusted the people to keep their promise to take only what they needed. And this they did. Well, most of them.

Osato was a woman who was never satisfied – she always wanted more. In fact, she was known for carrying around her own spoon, which she had tucked away in her headscarf – just in case she felt hungry! And on that day, when she laid eyes on all the food spread out on the tables before her, she couldn't control herself.

First, she gulped down a handful of noon-yellow, pineapple flavoured sky; then slurped away at some warm and spicy, sky stew. She was already stuffed, but loosened her robe, determined to devour anything she could lay her spoon on. She eyed some slices of pink and glistening morning sky, and quickly wolfed them down.

At last, when she had eaten her fill and the tables were empty, Osato waddled home. She was ready to burst but kept looking longingly at the sky, her mouth watering, wondering what new and delicious flavours it would taste of now – was it citrus storms or luscious mango? Perhaps it was honey sunset? She knew she wasn't supposed to take more than she needed but she couldn't resist any longer and out came her trusty spoon.

'Surely it can't hurt to take a little more? The sky is huge, after all,' she said with her mouth full of sky. She took another bite. And then another.

Finally, she threw aside her spoon and used her hands to scoop out a great piece of sky, far too much for one person to eat on their own. She took a small bite and chewed it slowly, realising that she had taken more than she could manage. The sky began to rumble; Osato was scared and knew that she couldn't waste it.

'What have I done?!' she cried.

At home she begged her family to help finish off the huge chunk of sky, but they were all too full from feasting all day! She asked her neighbours, but they only groaned at the sight of more food. She had no choice but to throw it away, and she told herself that there could be no harm in wasting just a little food. Deep down, she knew her actions had been wrong.

The next day, the people despaired for the sky withheld his food from them. Not even the cries of the children moved him, and he merely sighed and lifted himself up high, above the trees and the mountains, far beyond the reach of the people. Osato, who sat on the ground weeping stricken with guilt, heard his final words:

'I gave you all the food you could ever need, but that still wasn't enough for you and you kept on taking. I am disgusted by your greed and will never return.'

'But what will we eat? Without food we will die,' Osato cried. But she was answered only by silence.

As Osato sobbed, her tears fell to the ground, and the Earth was moved to pity.

'Do not weep,' she said gently, 'I will feed you. But you must work for your living and learn to harvest crops. Don't forget this lesson – take only what you need and not more and I will give you all I can.'

Osato and the people of Earth were overjoyed, and promised never to waste food ever, ever again.

Rewritten from the Nigerian folktale

Task 3: Interactive oral

You will engage in a discussion with your teacher on food. Before you begin, use the prompts and take some time to find some images on the internet that will help you during your presentation.

You are expected to speak for 3–4 minutes.

- Do you like to cook?
- Is food important in your culture?
- Do you think people enjoy food as much as they should?
- What time do you usually eat dinner?
- Are there any types of food you don't like?
- **Describe** a restaurant that you like to use. You should say:
  - □ where this restaurant is
  - □ what kind of food it serves
  - □ how often you go there
  - □ why you like eating there so much.

Reflection

In this chapter we have explored our exciting and complex relationship with food. We have considered where our food comes from and how we can help those who don't have enough of it. In addition we have evaluated the importance of the **context** food provides for **personal and cultural expression** and how important it is in shaping our **identities** and binding us to others.

Use this table to reflect on your own learning in this chapter.					
Questions we asked	**Answers we found**	**Any further questions now?**			
Factual: Where does our food come from? What effect does the food we eat have on our health?					
Conceptual: What does the food we eat tell us about who we are? How does food help shape who we are and how we live? How can we ensure that choices we make about food don't have harmful consequences?					
Debatable: Can we feed the world? Do we waste too much food?					
Approaches to learning you used in this chapter:	Description – what new skills did you learn?	How well did you master the skills?			
		Novice	Learner	Practitioner	Expert
Communication skills					
Collaboration skills					
Affective skills					
Information literacy skills					
Critical-thinking skills					
Creative-thinking skills					
Learner profile attribute(s)	Reflect on the importance of being balanced for your learning in this chapter.				
Balanced					

4 How can we find our way?

○ Exploration allows us to better understand our **orientation in space and time**, and make **connections** to others through experiencing the **context** of their lives.

CONSIDER THESE QUESTIONS:

Factual: What do you need to know in order to find your way? What skills do you need to help you survive if you get lost in the wilderness? Why don't animals get lost?

Conceptual: What should you do if you lose your way? How can we find our way back if we get lost? How can we help others find their way?

Debatable: Is getting lost always such a bad thing? Is it virtually impossible to get lost in today's world? Which learner profile attributes would help me find my way?

Now **share and compare** your thoughts and ideas with your partner, or with the whole class.

○ IN THIS CHAPTER WE WILL ...

■ **Find out** how we can find our way when we are lost.
■ **Explore** how others have coped when they have lost their way.
■ **Take action** to raise awareness about how we can be safe when we are in new places and help others to find their way.

These Approaches to Learning (ATL) skills will be useful …

- Communication skills
- Affective skills
- Information literacy skills
- Critical-thinking skills
- Creative-thinking skills

We will reflect on this learner profile attribute …

- **Thinker** – we use critical and creative thinking skills to analyse and take responsible action on complex problems.

Assessment opportunities in this chapter:

- **Criterion A**: Listening
- **Criterion B**: Reading
- **Criterion C**: Speaking
- **Criterion D**: Writing

THINK–SHARE–PAIR

Take two minutes to list some equipment that people can use to find their way.

Get into groups of three and share your list of equipment. Note down any items you don't have written down.

As a group, **discuss** each item and, using a table like the one below, rank the items in order of usefulness, placing the best at the top. Make sure you can **justify** your choices. You must **all agree as a group** on your choices.

Equipment	What does it do?	Explanation for ranking

KEY WORDS

bearings	migration
compass	navigation
directions	orientation

What skills do I need to help me survive if I get lost in the wilderness?

HOW WILL I KNOW WHERE I AM?

There's nothing more exciting than being in a new place. Meeting new people, discovering new foods, perhaps even having to communicate in a new language. But it can be scary too … especially if you lose your way.

We've all been there. Walking along, lost in thought, far too excited to pay attention to where you are going. And then, quite suddenly, that feeling of panic begins to grow inside you when you realize that you've passed that same water fountain at least a dozen times now, or even worse, that nothing around you looks familiar anymore. Ring any bells? Luckily for most of us we are either quickly rescued or we somehow find our bearings and make our way back to our family and friends.

But, we shouldn't let the possibility of losing our way put us off exploring new places. These new places bring us opportunities to make connections with others and this can be an incredibly enriching experience.

Instead, we need to know exactly what to do if we do get lost, and this chapter aims to help us become safer and better informed travellers.

ℹ Wilderness: describes a place where people do not live because the conditions there are too harsh

How would you cope if you were to lose your way in the wilderness? Would you know whether to keep moving or to stay put in the hope that someone might find you? Would you know which direction to walk in or how to find a source of clean drinking water? Where would you have learnt these survival skills?

'The television' may seem like an unlikely answer, but that's exactly where 14-year-old American teenager Jake Denham acquired the skills that would keep him alive when he became stranded on a mountain. You could say that television saved his life!

Over the past couple of decades, our appetite for reality TV shows has grown, and we've seen a rise in programmes with a strong survival or adventure element. One of the most popular adventurers to hit our screens is Bear Grylls. Admired by old and young alike, Grylls's no-nonsense approach and practical survival skills have gripped audiences across the globe.

From Grylls and other notable television personalities we've learnt how to find and forage for food, how to traverse difficult landscapes, how to cope in extreme weather conditions and, of course, how to find our way back when we get lost.

But, should television really be the source of this kind of information? Can we apply the skills we learn about on TV to real-life situations?

■ Bear Grylls

ACTIVITY: The Lost Boy

■ ATL

Communication skills: Make inferences and draw conclusions

Watch the following video from abc News and answer the questions that follow.

http://abcnews.go.com/US/teen-survives-reality-tv-widerness-skills/story?id=12524850

1 **Why were Jake and his family in the mountains?**
2 **How long was Jake stranded for?**
3 **What was the temperature that day?**
4 **The phrase 'veered off' means:**
   a **to fall down**
   b **to change direction**
   c **to get lost.**
5 **How did Jake get down the mountain?**
6 **What did he do next?**
7 **Which television programmes does he say he learnt these skills from?**
8 **What signs did he use to find his way back?**
9 **How did he feel?**

In groups, **discuss** the following:
• **How do you feel about Jake's experience?**
• **Should all children and teenagers be taught survival skills?**
• **Who is responsible for teaching children these skills?**
• **Should survival skills be taught at school?**

◆ Assessment opportunities

In this activity you have practised skills that are assessed using Criterion A: Listening.

ACTIVITY: Where am I?

Orienteering is a growing sport that could potentially save your life. During activities, participants are usually required to locate a number of features within a given time frame, using only a map and a compass. There is a strong focus on teamwork, and people who take part often become more athletic and develop better navigational skills.

Look at the multi-modal text above. It is a poster from the South African Orienteering Federation, an organization dedicated to the sport. The federation strives hard to to make orienteering accessible to wider audiences and runs a number of courses and events year round, for people of all ages.

The image in the poster is an allusion to *Lost,* an American television series about a group of plane-crash survivors who find themselves stranded on a desert island.

Look carefully at the poster and answer the following questions:

1 Who do you think is the target audience for the poster?
2 How do the creators use humour to engage their audience?
3 How does the text relate to the image in the poster?
4 Copy and complete the table below to **identify** an example of each of the following language features and comment on the effect:

Language feature	Example from poster	Effect
Modal auxiliary		
Interrogative sentence		
Imperative		
Adjective/s		

5 How effective do you think the poster is? **Explain** your answer.

Is it *virtually* impossible to get lost in today's world?

HOW CAN TECHNOLOGY HELP ME FIND MY WAY?

In the olden days, losing your way was no laughing matter. It could mean the difference between life and death. If you strayed too far from home, you could have ended up in the jaws of a predatory beast or risked dying of thirst. Scary! Our ancestors relied on the environment to help them find their way. They used the positions of the sun or the stars to figure out where they were, which is apparently as good as using any compass!

In literature people always seem to have the most creative ways of finding their way back home. In *The Wonderful Wizard of Oz*, Dorothy is advised to follow 'the Road of Yellow Bricks'; in the fairytale *Hansel and Gretel*, Hansel very resourcefully leaves a trail of breadcrumbs to help guide him and his little sister back from the dark depths of the forest.

In the past our survival was dependent on our ability to read the environment and pay attention to our surroundings. In today's world however, very few of us could boast about being able to find our way using the signs of nature. But that doesn't seem to worry us. Why?

We live in an age when advancements made in science and technology mean that we have many tools at our disposal for the purposes of navigation. In a world of satellite navigation systems and smartphones, with maps and directions available at the touch of a button, it is nearly impossible to get lost.

Nearly. Would we be able to cope if we were in a situation where we couldn't reach for our phones? Could our reliance on technology pose problems?

▼ Links to: Individuals and societies – Geography

It's in the stars!

The North Star, or Polaris, sits directly over the North Pole. If you manage to spot it, you can expect to find your way home in no time!

For centuries, people have relied on the natural world to provide us with directional signs. Whether it's the earth, the sea or the sky that provides us with these clues, we cannot deny that they are all around us. A comforting thought, if we ever find ourselves lost without a compass, map or fancy gadget! But how many of us actually know how to read these signs?

Ordnance Survey pride themselves on being Britain's national mapping authority and use their blog to discuss all things geography, Geographic Information (GI) and map related.

Follow the link below and see if you can figure out how to use the stars to find your bearings.

https://www.ordnancesurvey.co.uk/blog/2011/08/forgotten-your-compass-use-the-stars-to-navigate/

Test yourself by explaining what you have learnt to a friend or family member.

ACTIVITY: The lost art of getting lost

ATL

Communication skills: Make inferences and draw conclusions

Read the following extract from a feature article from the BBC online magazine.

Once you have read the article, see if you can complete the following tasks:

1 **Summarize** the content of the article in one or two sentences.
2 Use a digital dictionary to find the definition of the words in blue.
3 Can you find any personal anecdotes in the text? Why might they have been included?

In pairs or groups of three, **discuss** the following questions:
- **How does the writer feel about using technology to find our way?**
- **What does he think are the problems of using technology for navigational purposes?**
- **Do you agree or disagree with the views expressed in the article?**
- **What do you think about the advice offered by Rebecca Solnit?**
- **Can you think of any other problems we could face if we become too dependent on technology for this purpose?**

Assessment opportunities

In this activity you have practised skills that are assessed using Criterion B: Reading and Criterion C: Speaking.

Adapted from the online magazine

The lost art of getting lost

Technology means maps and directions are constantly at hand, and getting lost is more unlikely than ever before. While for many this is a thing of joy, Stephen Smith asks if we may be missing out.

When was the last time you were well and truly lost? Chances are it's been a while. Extraordinary gadgets like smartphones and satnavs let us pinpoint our location unerringly. Like the people in Downton Abbey, we all know our place.

However, the technology that delivers the world into the palms of our hands may be ushering in a kind of social immobility.

Discovery used to mean going out and coming across stuff – now it seems to mean turning inwards and gazing at screens. We've become reliant on machines to help us get around, so much so that it's changing the way we behave, particularly among younger people who have no experience of a time before GPS.

This saves a lot of confusion, of course. If we totted up how much of our lives we used to spend getting lost before the internet, it would be almost as long as it takes to sit through a Netflix series.

But still, can we stop for a moment to work out where we are, if only for old times' sake? I have misgivings about what we forfeit by never being lost.

When I think of my happiest adventures in foreign parts, they've often been after wandering off the beaten track, like the time I stumbled on the rudimentary boxing gym in the stews of old Havana where the Cubans produce Olympic champions.

Rebecca Solnit, author of A Field Guide to Getting Lost, says the answer to our distracted, information-saturated times is to get away from it all.

'Go some place you've never been before,' she says. 'I just came back from the Alaskan Arctic, deep in the authentic wild, with bears, moose and elk. We were more than a hundred miles from the nearest road or settlement.'

Or phone signal. Closer to home, technology blinds us to our surroundings in ways we don't even notice, says the writer Will Self.

'GPS tells you exactly where you are but it doesn't orient you at all. We come out of a Tube station or get off a bus or we're in an unfamiliar town, we pull out our phones and we get lost at that point.'

Downton Abbey: a popular British television series set in the early twentieth century

GPS: Global Positioning System, a space-based navigation system that provides us with location and time information

Netflix: an online provider that allows you to stream movies and television programmes

In literature, characters seem to get lost all the time!

Below are some quotes about some well-loved characters who have lost their way.

THINK–PAIR–SHARE

In pairs or groups, **discuss** these quotes about getting lost and finding your way. Think about the following:

- **Interpret** what each quote means.?
- **Which attitudes are being expressed in these quotes?**
- **Which one do you like the most? Explain** why.

◆ Assessment opportunities

In this activity you have practised skills that are assessed using Criterion B: Reading and Criterion C: Speaking.

One day Alice came to a fork in the road and saw a Cheshire cat in a tree. 'Which road do I take?' she asked.

'Where do you want to go?' was his response.

'I don't know,' Alice answered.

'Then,' said the cat, 'it doesn't matter.'

■ Lewis Carroll, from *Alice's Adventures in Wonderland*

'If we walk far enough,' said Dorothy, 'we shall sometime come to some place.'

■ L. Frank Baum, from *The Wonderful Wizard of Oz*

Which learner profile attributes would help me find my way?

WHAT QUALITIES DOES A GREAT EXPLORER NEED TO HAVE?

As humans, our insatiable curiosity and thirst for adventure has always driven us to seek out the unknown. For centuries we have ventured out to the far corners of the Earth in the search for knowledge, for power, for a better life and new opportunities.

One of the greatest consequences of exploration has been the wonderful prospect of making connections with people from other places. These connections have enhanced our lives in ways we could never have imagined. Through connecting with others over time, we have changed our perspectives, developed our language, transformed our diets and enriched our cultures with what we have learnt.

■ An astrolabe

Sadly, not all expeditions have ended as positively as we would like to believe; too many explorers in the past, blinded by ambition and a desire for power, have caused more damage than good.

So, how can we separate good explorers from bad ones? What characteristics must explorers possess if they are to be successful at finding their way, surviving in and adapting to new surroundings *and*, most importantly, making positive connections wherever they go?

■ Explorers in the past would have needed to use maps like these to navigate

English for the IB MYP 1: *by Concept*

▼ Links to: Individuals and societies – History

Discovering the New World – The Age of Exploration

Although the story of exploration doesn't begin here, it was during the late fifteenth century when explorers from Spain, France, England and the Netherlands developed a taste for travel and an urgent need to make sense of their world. And it was on the New World that they came to set their sights.

These epic voyages were aided by technological innovations of the time; such as the astrolabe, a device used to calculate latitude; the carvel, a small, fast ship; and the magnetic compass.

These voyages brought wealth and prosperity to the nations to which the explorers belonged but had tragic consequences for the indigenous (native) populations who were already thriving in the New World.

For more information about the history of exploration, including facts about famous explorers from across the globe, visit **The Mariners' Museum** website. It will also help you with your next task!

■ Christopher Columbus arriving in America

Synonyms

One of the best ways to enrich your writing is through varying your vocabulary and synonyms are by far the easiest way to do this.

A synonym is a word that means exactly or nearly the same as another word in the same language.

For example:
• The adjectives *large, huge, colossal* and *enormous* are all synonyms for the word *big*.
• The verbs *step, stride, stroll* and *amble* are all synonyms for the word *walk*.

Meet the thesaurus

A thesaurus is simply a dictionary of synonyms and an invaluable companion for those studying English. Why not ask your teacher to lend you one? Or, you'll most certainly be able to find one online or in your school library.

Once you get your hands on one, see how many synonyms you can find for some of the words you use most often in your writing.

ACTIVITY: The world's greatest explorer

■ ATL

Information literacy skills: Access information to be informed and inform others

So, how well-rounded were the world's most notorious explorers? It's time to find out!

Let's start with Charles Darwin. Although today we remember Darwin for his work as a naturalist, his most famous findings were the result of a five-year-long voyage he embarked upon in 1831. During this journey aboard the *HMS Beagle*, Darwin carried out extensive research on the specimens of flora and fauna he collected from across the globe.

■ Charles Darwin, National Portrait Gallery, London

Charles Darwin – Learner Profile

General information: Born 1809, Shrewsbury, England. Died 1882, London, England

Learner profile attributes: knowledgeable; inquirer; open-minded; risk-taker

Evidence:

Knowledgable – Darwin attended two of the most prestigious universities in the country. His work spans three sciences – zoology, botany and geology. He is well known for being one of the most famous scientists in history and his work has changed the way we think about many things.

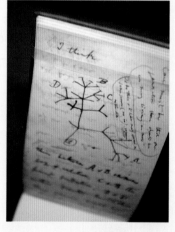

■ Some sketches by Darwin

Inquirer – Darwin's natural curiosity led him to give up studying medicine and work towards uncovering the mysteries of the natural world. He carried out hands-on research and experiments on the many specimens he gathered during his expeditions.

Open-minded and risk-taker – Sadly, people living in Darwin's world weren't as open to new ideas as we are today. Darwin was incredibly open-minded and challenged the way people thought about certain issues. He took a great risk in presenting his theories about evolution in his groundbreaking and controversial book on evolutionary theory, *On the Origin of Species* (1859). People were shocked and Darwin became the subject of ridicule in the London newspapers.

MR. BERGH TO THE RESCUE.

THE DEFRAUDED GORILLA. "That *Man* wants to claim my Pedigree. He says he is one of my Descendants."

Mr. BERGH. "Now, Mr. DARWIN, how could you insult him so?"

■ Cartoon of Darwin

naturalist: an expert in or student of natural history

embarked: from the verb 'embark', which means to begin something or to go on board a ship or aircraft

flora: plants

fauna: animals

controversial: something that causes disagreement and discussion

evolutionary theory: the theory that suggests that living organisms developed from earlier forms during the history of the Earth

prestigious: respected or admired

Based on what you've just read about Darwin, do you think he was a good explorer?

Do you know any other famous explorers? Do you have a favourite explorer? Or a least favourite explorer? Do you know any famous explorers from your own country? Or perhaps explorers that came to your country from other places?

In pairs, conduct some research about an explorer of your choice and deliver an engaging presentation to your class. You can make a poster or put together a computer slideshow. Try to speak for at least three minutes.

Use the following questions to help you organize your research and presentation.

- **Who was your explorer and where did they live? What do you know about their personality?**
- **When was your explorer active? When did their most famous expeditions take place?**
- **What did they set out to discover?**
- **How did they undertake their journey/s? Did they encounter any obstacles?**
- **Were their voyage/s successful?**
- **What learner profile attributes does your explorer have? Which do they lack? Make sure you can provide evidence to support your choices.**

EXTENSION

In addition to your presentation, you could create a learner profile for your explorer like the one on page 82.

◆ Assessment opportunities

In this activity you have practised skills that are assessed using Criterion B: Reading and Criterion C: Speaking.

Why don't animals get lost?

In December 2015, a family in Berlin got the best Christmas present ever when their cat Miko returned home after seven years! Other than being 'a bit too thin' Miko was safe, healthy and extremely happy to be reunited with her loving owners. But how did she do it?

Have you ever wondered how animals rarely seem to lose their way? Every year, millions of animals worldwide embark on epic journeys across land, sea and sky and yet somehow always manage to find their way home. Perhaps we as humans can learn a thing or two from the animal kingdom!

■ Miko the cat reunited with her owner after seven long years

ⓘ Did you know that:

- in its lifetime, an Arctic tern will cover the same distance it would take to travel to the moon and back *three times*!
- each year over a million wildebeest migrate from the Serengeti in Tanzania to the Masai Mara in Kenya
- every year the inhabitants of Christmas Island are paid a visit by over 50 million red crabs on their way to the sea to lay their eggs.

■ Birds migrating

ROAD CLOSED
RED CRAB MIGRATION
NO ENTRY BY VEHICLES
BEYOND THIS POINT

■ Crabs migrating

WATCH–THINK–SHARE

ATL

Information literacy skills: Access information to be informed and inform others

Earth Juice is a series of weekly videos, which explores the wonders of the natural world. Watch the following video and listen carefully to what Chris Howard says about how animals find their way: www.youtube.com/watch?v=kW7jhE1v7Ls.

As you watch, answer the following questions:

1 **According to Howard, how are cape vultures finding their way?**
2 **What other man-made structures are helping animals during their travels?**
3 **List some of the methods animals use to find their way.**
4 **Which equipment used by humans does Howard compare some of these methods to?**

Now, share your answers with a partner/group and discuss what you have learnt from the video.

◆ Assessment opportunities

In this activity you have practised skills that are assessed using Criterion A: Listening.

Animal idioms

In the video, Howard uses the idiom 'on the wing', which means flying or in flight. There are many, many animal-inspired idioms in the English language, including the following:

- *One swallow doesn't make a summer* – You should not assume that something is true just because you have seen one piece of evidence for it. Swallows returning to a place often signifies the start of summer, but just seeing one doesn't guarantee that the season has officially started.
- *As blind as a bat* – blind; unable to see. Bats are known for their blindness.
- *Like a fish out of water* – being out of place or feeling uncomfortable. You would expect fish to feel very uncomfortable when out of water!

Can you guess what the following idioms might mean? Check your answer by searching for them online:

- *His bark is worse than his bite.*
- *She eats like a horse.*
- *What's the matter, cat got your tongue?*

Do you know any animal idioms from your own culture or country? What do they mean? Share them with your group and see if you can find any similarities between them.

ACTIVITY: The incredible journey

■ ATL

Communication skills: Read critically and for comprehension

Luath, Bodger and Tao are the loveable protagonists in Sheila Burnford's 1961 novel *The Incredible Journey*. Together, the unlikely companions (two dogs and a shrewd Siamese cat) embark upon a remarkable adventure in which they travel over 3,000 miles to find their way home to their beloved owners.

Here is a short extract from the novel in which Luath, the young Labrador, chooses a trail along which to continue their journey. Read it carefully and then can complete these tasks.

1 **Identify** the time of day the extract is set.
2 **Find** a word in the text which means 'group of three'?
3 **Think back** to the Earth Juice video you watched earlier. Can you make any connections between the video and this extract? (Clues: logging trail; ruts)
4 **Find** a word in the extract that is a synonym for 'hidden'.
5 Luath relies on his instincts to decide which way to go. **Find** an example from the extract that shows this.
6 What season do you think it is?
7 Which learner profile attributes do you think Luath possesses? Copy and complete the table below. For each attribute, find evidence from the text to **justify** your explanation.

In the grey light of dawn the trio continued down the side of the road until they reached a point where it took a right-angled turn. Here they hesitated before a **disused logging** trail that led **westward** from the side of the road, its entrance almost concealed by overhanging branches. The leader lifted his head and appeared almost as though he were searching for the **scent** of something, some reassurance; and apparently he found it, for he led his companions up the trail between the overhanging trees. The going here was softer; the middle was overgrown with grass and the **ruts** on either side were full of dead leaves. The close-growing trees which almost met overhead would afford more shade when the sun rose higher. These were all considerations that the old dog needed, for he had been tired today even before he started, and his pace was already considerably slower.

Learner profile attribute	Explanation	Evidence (quote)

◆ Assessment opportunities

In this activity you have practised skills that are assessed using Criterion B: Reading.

Is getting lost always such a bad thing?

Sometimes we stumble upon the most extraordinary things when we've lost our way and historically some of our greatest discoveries were made completely by accident! Have you ever found anything interesting when you've lost your way? Perhaps you've found something you weren't even looking for?

But I'm sure you'd agree, that in today's world, it's becoming increasingly harder to get lost – both physically and metaphorically. We've already seen how technology has made it almost impossible to lose our way, but is it putting something even greater at risk?

When was the last time you had the chance to lose yourself in your own thoughts? Or get lost in a good book? In a world where we are surrounded by screens, it can be hard to tear your eyes away from them even for a moment.

But wouldn't it be nice if we could just switch off for a short while? Perhaps we might find something new!

LISTEN–THINK–SHARE

ATL

Communication skills: Take effective notes in class

Listen to the song 'Let's get Lost' by Graham Gouldman, who is an English songwriter and musician. Gouldman was inspired to write the song after being interviewed for a BBC Radio 4 documentary called 'The Loss of Lostness'.

www.bbc.co.uk/programmes/p034sdhd

As you listen:
- **Make some notes about how Gouldman feels about getting lost.**
- **Identify why Gouldman thinks that getting lost is not always such a bad thing.**
- **Consider what the problems of Gouldman's message might be.**
- **In pairs, discuss what the implications are of never truly being lost.**

Hint

If you need to remind yourself on how to make effective notes, take a look at page 53 in Chapter 3.

◆ Assessment opportunities

In this activity you have practised skills that are assessed using Criterion A: Listening.

ACTIVITY: Lovely labyrinths and amazing mazes

ℹ **maze:** a series of paths and hedges designed as a puzzle through which you have to find your way

labyrinth: a more complicated series of paths or passages, which makes it difficult to find your way

Today, we often use the terms *maze* and *labyrinth* interchangeably.

According to Greek legend, King Minos, who lived on the island of Crete, had a colossal maze built under his palace in which to keep a monster called the minotaur. The minotaur was a hideous creature, half human and half bull, that needed human flesh in order to stay alive. Every year, young men and women from a neighbouring kingdom would be let loose in the maze as sacrifices for the monster. The maze was incredibly intricate and the poor men and women would become hopelessly lost and eventually eaten.

The minotaur was finally defeated by a man called Theseus, who volunteered to be placed in the maze. Theseus slew the monster and then used a trail of twine he had cleverly laid down when he entered the maze to help him find his way out.

In the ancient world, labyrinths served an important function: either to keep something in or to keep unwelcome visitors out! By the end of the sixteenth

■ The maze at Reignac-sur-Indre, France, is called the largest plant maze in the world

English for the IB MYP 1: *by Concept*

century, however, we had decided that actually, getting lost could be quite thrilling and people began to install mazes in their gardens for pleasure and entertainment.

Mazes were not only giant puzzles that could provide hours of enjoyment to those brave enough to get lost among the hedges, but could also be private spaces where you could escape for a moment's peace and quiet. Mazes don't just exist in gardens, but have become a popular feature of puzzle books too.

The story of the Cretan labyrinth is by far the most popular, but mazes have resurfaced time and time again in stories and films and continue to captivate our imagination today. Can you think of any stories or films that have featured mazes?

Now **design** your own maze. Remember, the more complicated it is, the harder it will be for people to find their way out!

If you need some help with creating your own puzzle, check out the following link.

http://puzzlemaker.discoveryeducation.com/AdvMazeSetupForm.asp

In the last chapter you learnt how to write a set of instructions. Why not put that skill into practice?

Write a set of instructions on how to find your way out of the maze you have designed.

If you get stuck, check out the tips on page 59 to help refresh your memory.

EXTENSION

Have you ever visited a garden that has a maze?

The breathtaking maze at the Palace of Versailles and the world famous one at Hampton Court Palace in England are just two among the thousands that exist worldwide.

Carry out some research about mazes in your home country.

You may want to address the following areas:
- The location of the maze – Where is it? Is it open to the public?
- The history of the maze – When was it created? Who commissioned it? Is there a story behind it?
- The structure of the maze – How was it made? How big is it? How long would it take to find your way out?
- Images of the maze – What does the maze look like? Are there any photographs or paintings available of the maze?

Share your findings with a partner.

◆ Assessment opportunities

In this activity you have practised skills that are assessed using Criterion D: Writing.

How can we help others find their way?

WHAT SHOULD I DO IF I WERE TO GET LOST?

Getting lost can be a very daunting experience to say the least. For young people in particular, it can be incredibly frightening. This is precisely why it's so important that we know what to do if we do lose our way. It is only when we have the knowledge that we need to find our own way, that we can help others to find theirs.

How well do you know your way around your local area? Do you use any particular features to help you figure out where you are? Perhaps there's a distinctive looking tree you know in your area? Or maybe you live near a particular landmark – your old school or a park that you sometimes visit – that can help you to identify your location? How familiar are you with the street names in your locality – maybe you use these to figure out how to get home?

These are all great ways to help you get a sense of your bearings, but what happens when you get lost in an unfamiliar place, further away from home? Would you know what to do? Do you know who to approach for help?

In this section, you will learn about what you should do if you get lost and how you can help others to find their way and keep safe.

Here, a reader from England shares her tips for travelling to the magnificent city of Istanbul in Turkey.

As you read, consider what techniques she uses to offer other readers advice.

The writer includes **factual information** which she presents using **declarative sentences** to add authenticity to her advice.

www.telegraph.co.uk/travel/yourtravels

She includes **opinions** and draws on her own **personal experiences** to help **justify** her advice.

She addresses the reader directly by using **personal pronouns** ('you').

Conditionals are also used to present alternatives and to vary her advice ('If you really want ...').

One of my favourite places in Istanbul is Eyup. **This is one of the holy places of Islam; the tomb of Eyup Ensari, a companion of the Prophet Mohammed**. It is a site of Islamic pilgrimage. **Take** the ferry from Eminonu up the Golden Horn, a great trip in itself. **Walk** up to the Eyup Camii and visit the tomb and mosque with the faithful. **It is a wonderfully moving and memorable experience. You** are always welcome but you **must** be respectful and follow strict dress codes (ladies **should** always carry a headscarf with them in Istanbul).

Continue your walk up to the beautiful Eyup cemetery **for wonderful views of the Golden Horn. If you really want to see Islamic Istanbul, don't just go to the Blue Mosque;** visit other mosques around the city, which are not full of visitors.

Reader, England

The writer uses **imperatives** ('take', 'walk') to instruct her audience on what to do when in Istanbul.

She uses **modal auxiliary verbs** to alter the tone of her piece – sometimes to soften her advice ('should') and at others to make it more assertive ('must').

■ Istanbul

Writing to advise

We can all do with some good advice once in a while.

When you give someone advice, you are providing them with some sensible guidance or are making recommendations, usually based on your own experiences.

Look at the extract from the *Telegraph* Online's 'Your Travel' section (on page 91) where readers can post information about their own travel experiences and offer useful advice to others.

Need some advice on how to advise? Here are some top tips:

- **Address your audience; make them feel involved** – don't forget to include personal pronouns and don't be afraid to throw in some questions. (Why don't you …?, Have you tried/thought about …?)
- **Use modal auxiliary verbs** – these can help soften your tone as you don't want to come across as too pushy! (You **should/could/ought** …, maybe you **could/can …,** perhaps you **should …)**
- **Be clear, direct and assertive** – this might contradict the last point slightly, but, in some cases, you will need to get your point across firmly. Use **imperatives** and **modal auxiliary verbs** like 'must' to achieve the desired effect.
- **Justify your advice** – make sure you provide **explanations** for all the advice you offer. After all, people want to know why they should do what you suggest.
- **Make it authentic** – include **personal anecdotes** and examples to prove that your advice is effective. What better evidence than your own personal experiences? It can also be useful to include **factual information** to show that you know what you are talking about.
- **Think carefully about the audience** – make sure you vary your language to suit your audience. You want your advice to be accessible and engaging.

ACTIVITY: Writing to advise

To begin, get into pairs or groups and **discuss** what you should do if you were to get lost.

Use the following questions to help guide your discussion:

- **What is the first thing you would do?**
- **Who would be the best person to approach for help?**
- **What information would you need in order to find your family/friends/way back?**
- **How might you be feeling and how do you think you should behave?**

KidPower is an American organization dedicated to educating parents and young people about how to keep safe at home, at school and when out and about.

Follow the link below and read the article: **www.kidpower.org/library/article/getting-lost/**.

As you read, consider the following:

- **Who is the article aimed at? How do you know?**
- **Does the advice in the article bear any similarities to the discussion you had in your group?**
- **What does the writer advise children to do if they get lost? Do you think this is good advice? Why or why not?**

Using the information you have gathered from your discussion and the article, create a poster advising children aged between seven and ten years old about what to do if they get lost in a public place.

Before you begin, think carefully about your **target audience**:

- **What kind of language and sentence types will you need to use to ensure that they understand your advice?**
- **How will you present it? What would appeal to young children?**

You should aim to include as many features of advisory writing as you can.

EXTENSION: READING THE SIGNS

What is the name of the street you live on? Have you ever wondered where that name comes from?

Streets are given particular names for all sorts of reasons – sometimes they are named after certain trades that may have taken place in the locality or after famous people who have in some way made a contribution to the area. Sometimes they are named to describe the landscape or after a certain landmark nearby.

Think about the name of your street. Are there any clues as to why it has been given this particular name?

Carry out some research about the name of your road ... who knows what you might discover!

Don't be afraid to contact your library or a local museum – they will be happy to help you.

Did you know that in some places the street signs reflect the diversity of the local community? East London's Bethnal Green is home to a large Bengali population who have been there since the seventeenth century. To celebrate their presence and contribution to society, the street signs in the area are written in Bengali script.

■ Brick Lane street sign

Take action: How can I make a difference?

! We can all make a small difference by raising awareness on what to do if you get lost.

! Take action ...

♦ By sharing the information you have learnt in this chapter with others. Perhaps you can display the poster you have created in a local school or your public library? Make sure you ask permission first.

♦ By raising awareness at your local school. Perhaps you can ask your teachers to talk about this in tutor period or even organize a whole school assembly?

! Good luck!

SOME SUMMATIVE TASKS TO TRY

Use these tasks to apply and extend your learning in this chapter. These tasks are designed so that you can evaluate your learning in the Language acquisition criteria.

THIS TASK CAN BE USED TO EVALUATE YOUR LEARNING IN CRITERION C TO CAPABLE LEVEL

Task 1: 'Lost' by Michael Rosen

- Answer the questions below.
- Use your own words as much as possible.
- Do not use translating devices or dictionaries for this task.

Watch the short video of Michael Rosen reading his poem 'Lost': **www.youtube.com/watch?v=n3Y7lFwkqg0**.

In groups of three or four, have a discussion about the content of the poem.

Here are some prompts that might help you:

1 What is the poem about?
2 What age group do you think it is aimed at? Why would it appeal to people of this age group?
3 How does Rosen present the feeling of being lost? Think about his use of language and the way in which he recites the poem (tone of voice, facial expressions).
4 Is it an accurate presentation? Have you experienced anything similar?
5 Does the way in which you react to being lost change as you get older or is being lost always as frightening?
6 What is your opinion about the poem?
7 How does it link to the issues explored in this chapter so far?

You must:

- Speak for 3–4 minutes as a group.
- Listen carefully to what others say and respond appropriately.
- Make sure you engage others in your group by asking questions.
- Try to vary your vocabulary and use of sentence types.

THIS TASK CAN BE USED TO EVALUATE YOUR LEARNING IN CRITERION B TO CAPABLE LEVEL

Task 2: Why did the orienteer cross the road?

- Answer the questions that follow, using your own words as much as possible.
- Do not use translating devices or dictionaries for this task.
- Refer as closely as possible to the multimodal text, justifying your answers and giving examples when asked.
- You will have 60 minutes to complete this task.

Look carefully at the poster on the left.

1 What kind of organization has produced this image and for what purpose?
2 How does the text in the poster link to the image?
3 How have the creators tried to make the poster eye-catching and appealing to viewers?
4 Who do you think is the target audience for this poster? **Explain** why.
5 **Interpret** the message this poster is trying to convey.
6 How has the message been presented in this poster? List the:
   a visual features
   b textual features.
7 Where might you expect to see a poster like this?
8 Why might it be useful to learn the skills that the organization is promoting?
9 Do you think it is important that young people learn these skills? **Explain** why. Are young people in your home country taught these skills? Are you aware of similar organizations in your home country?
10 Which learner profile attributes do you think orienteers need to possess?

Reflection

In this chapter we have explored the skills and knowledge we need in order to find our way back home if we were ever to get lost and have a better understanding of our **orientation in space and time**. We have also looked at how we can offer advice to others and help them stay safe and find their way back in similar **contexts**. Although for most people getting lost is a frightening prospect, we have discovered that, for some, it can be an exciting opportunity to discover something new, escape for a while or make **connections** with others. We've looked at how it is important to be explorers and challenge ourselves, but also how crucial it is to ensure that we never compromise our safety in the process.

Use this table to reflect on your own learning in this chapter.					
Questions we asked	Answers we found	Any further questions now?			
Factual: What do you need to know in order to find your way? What skills do you need to help you survive if you get lost in the wilderness? Why don't animals get lost?					
Conceptual: What should you do if you lose your way? How can we find our way back if we get lost? How can we help others find their way?					
Debatable: Is getting lost always such a bad thing? Is it virtually impossible to get lost in today's world? Which learner profile attributes would help me find my way?					
Approaches to learning you used in this chapter:	Description – what new skills did you learn?	How well did you master the skills?			
		Novice	Learner	Practitioner	Expert
Communication skills					
Affective skills					
Information literacy skills					
Critical-thinking skills					
Creative-thinking skills					
Learner profile attribute(s)	Reflect on the importance of being a thinker for your learning in this chapter.				
Thinker					

⑤ What would life be like in a world without letters?

○ A carefully written letter can **communicate** a **message** to an **audience** that can help strengthen our **identities and relationships**.

CONSIDER THESE QUESTIONS:

Factual: Why do we write letters? What makes a good letter?

Conceptual: How can letters help bring us closer together? What do letters reveal about the past? How have letters influenced literature, art and culture? Why are letters important?

Debatable: In an age of digital communication, is the art of letter writing at risk of dying out?

Now **share and compare** your thoughts and ideas with your partner, or with the whole class.

○ IN THIS CHAPTER WE WILL ...

- **Find out** how to write letters for different purposes.
- **Explore** how letter writing has changed over time.
- **Take action** to revive the art of letter writing and reach out to others by becoming a pen pal.

These Approaches to Learning (ATL) skills will be useful …

- Communication skills
- Collaboration skills
- Reflection skills
- Information literacy skills
- Critical-thinking skills
- Creative-thinking skills

We will reflect on this learner profile attribute …

Communicator – we express ourselves confidently and creatively in many ways.

Assessment opportunities in this chapter:

- ◆ **Criterion A**: Listening
- ◆ **Criterion B**: Reading
- ◆ **Criterion C**: Speaking
- ◆ **Criterion D**: Writing

Did you know that the first recorded handwritten letter dates as far back as 500 BCE? It was written by the Persian Queen Atossa, most likely using leaves and bark from trees, which were considered quite advanced writing materials at the time!

DISCUSS

Get into pairs or groups of three, and use a search engine to carry out some research about other materials used for writing letters over the ages. Or just find out more about the history of letter writing.

What did you find?

In your groups create a timeline documenting the history of writing. Don't be afraid to include pictures!

KEY WORDS

analogue	formal
correspondence	informal
epistle	recipient
epistolary	salutations
etiquette	telegram

Why are letters important?

WHAT CAN WE LEARN FROM WRITING LETTERS?

There's something quite magical about receiving a letter in the post. The excitement you experience on seeing the familiar handwriting of a loved one on the envelope is replaced only by the delicious pleasure of tearing it open and devouring each and every word of the letter inside.

Once a necessary tool used for communicating with people over long distances, the humble letter has become more than just a way for us to keep in touch. Letters can help us build bridges and make connections with others; they have the power to bring us closer together and help us express ourselves when our voices fail us in face-to-face situations. Letters allow us to share news, experiences, ideas and even secrets. Letters provide us with a private space for personal reflection – we can learn a great deal about ourselves through the process of writing. It is through letters that literacy, our ability to read and write, will eventually be kept alive.

But sadly, in recent years we have seen a decline in letter writing, and today most of the letters that we receive are official communications rather than personal messages from friends and family. Some people think this is a tragedy as we have so much to lose if the art of letter writing dies out completely.

Many argue, however, that letter writing isn't dying but has changed into something greater. In a world of technological advancement, digital communication and instant messaging, such as emails and text messages, are replacing the written letter. Although such developments have had a positive impact on the way in which we communicate today, letters offer a degree of privacy that emails and other forms of digital communication do not and perhaps we are risking more than we know.

In this chapter we will explore the importance of letters and their contribution to our culture of communication. We will consider how letters can help us understand the past and how they have the power to bring us closer together. We will also examine the changing world of communication and whether the art of letter writing may still thrive.

When was the last time you received a letter in the post? Or wrote a letter yourself?

THINK–PAIR–SHARE

'In the first place let us draw what all letter-writers instinctively draw, a sketch of the person to whom the letter is addressed. Without someone warm and breathing on the other side of the page, letters are worthless.' – *Virginia Woolf,* Three Guineas

Virginia Woolf was an important voice in British literature during the early twentieth century. She was known for her fiction and essays, and wrote many letters during her lifetime.

Read the quote above about letter writing and complete the following tasks. **Discuss** your responses with a partner.

1 **Interpret** what Woolf means. Use a dictionary to check that you understand every word. Can you **explain** it in your own words?
2 Do you agree with Woolf?
3 **Evaluate** whether letters reveal as much about the recipient as they do about the writer.
4 Is it necessary to know the person you are writing to, or can you write to someone you might not know? Can you think of any situations in which you may be required to write a letter to someone you don't know?
5 **Discuss** how this would affect the way you might write your letter. Would you think more carefully about your language choices when writing?

Why do we write letters?

DISCUSS

So why do people write letters? In pairs or groups of three, create a mind-map of all the reasons people may have for writing letters.

What did you come up with?

Here are some ideas you could add:
- **to inform or explain**
- **to describe**
- **to persuade or to make a request**
- **to advise**
- **to complain.**

WHAT ARE THE CONVENTIONS OF A GOOD LETTER?

We began writing letters as soon as we learnt how to put pen to paper. Humans have always thrived on interaction with others and for a long time the letter was an almost indispensable tool for communication.

There are so many reasons why we write – letters can be used to record and pass on information; they can be used to express complex ideas to which the spoken word might not always be able to do justice. Sometimes we can use letters to help ease difficult situations or to fulfil specific, practical purposes. Often, we write to one another for the sheer pleasure of it and to maintain important relationships with our loved ones.

Although many of us would like nothing more than to pick up a pen and let our words flow out on to paper, letters have a very specific structure and there are certain conventions we need to follow if we want our message to be communicated effectively.

We need to know a number of things before we even begin to think about writing; Who am I writing to? How well do I know them? For what purpose am I writing this letter? What do I want to achieve? Only when we have this information, can we afford to start constructing our letter.

Formal or informal?

Most letters fall into one of two categories. The formality of a letter depends on a number of factors including the purpose of the letter and who the intended recipient is. Here is a simple guide, which should help you determine whether a letter is formal or informal.

Informal letters:
- are usually addressed to family or friends – you might write one to your grandmother or your best friend
- employ a friendly, casual and sometimes conversational tone
- are written using simple language and a variety of sentence moods
- often use sobriquets (nicknames) when referring to the recipient.

Formal letters:
- are usually addressed to people you may be less familiar with, including those in positions of authority, for example, your headteacher
- have a clearly defined purpose and often have a very specific layout
- use formal terms of address and titles to refer to the recipient
- are written using more sophisticated language and are often organized using discourse markers.

In formal letters the salutation (your initial greeting and how your letter begins) determines the sign-off (how you end your letter). If your letter begins with 'Dear Sir/Madam' you must sign off with the words 'Yours faithfully'. This is to establish trust, as you and the recipient are unlikely to have met in person. If you begin with the name or title of a person such as 'Dear Mr Dickens' you should sign-off with the words 'Yours sincerely'.

READ–THINK–WRITE

Look at the two letters on pages
104–105 and complete the
following tasks.

1 Which letter do you think is informal? Which one is formal? Find
   evidence to support your answer.
2 **Identify** the purpose of each letter.
3 Who is the recipient in each case? How are they addressed by
   the writer? What kind of relationship do you think they have with
   the writer?
4 **Identify** the parts of each letter. What are the conventions of
   formal and informal letters? Can you **summarize** the purpose of
   each individual paragraph?
5 **Find** some similarities and differences between the two letters.

◆ Assessment opportunities

In this activity you have practised skills that are assessed using
Criterion B: Reading.

EXTENSION

What techniques are used by each writer to
achieve the purpose of the letter? For the
first letter you might want to refresh your
memory by re-reading pages 92–3.

Now that we've had a look at some examples,
let's have a go at writing our own letters!

To prepare, in pairs or groups of three,
look at the following scenarios. All of these
require a letter to be written. **Discuss** each
one and copy and complete the table below.

Scenario	Who is the intended recipient?	What is the purpose for writing?	Should this be a formal or informal letter?	Additional notes
Your best friend has won the national lottery				
You don't like the food in your school canteen				
You have seen a particular item that you would like for your birthday				
You have received a fine from your local library for a book you returned months ago				

On your own, choose **one** of the scenarios
and **write a short letter**. You can use the
additional notes section in the table to do
some planning first.

Once you've finished, swap your letter
with someone else and get them to spot
how many **conventions** you've managed to
include. Do the same with their letter.

ⓘ A discourse marker is a word or phrase used to link
written ideas. Discourse markers can help make your
writing clearer and more cohesive.

Examples include: *and, next, for instance, because,
similarly, however and whereas.*

445 Mount Eden Road
Auckland

15th May 2015

Dearest Liz,

How are you? Thank you so much for the invitation. Of course I'll come to your birthday party! Has it been a year already? How time flies! Have you made all the arrangements? If not, perhaps I can give you some advice – I plan parties all the time!

I expect by now you've sent out all of your invitations? Who else have you invited? I'm so curious to know! I hope Gustavo and Yeva are coming – they're always great fun at a party. Have you thought about the food you'll be serving? Maybe you could have some finger food or canapes for your guests to nibble on? Oh, and make sure you don't forget to cater for the vegetarians. I remember last year at my leaving party there wasn't a vegetable in sight, and poor Tom had to go home hungry! What a disaster! Well, that taught me a lesson! Have you thought about having a theme for your party? I think you should go for a tropical theme as it'll be just the thing to get us into the mood for summer now that the weather is finally getting better! If you still need decorations I know a great place where you can buy some online; I suggest you visit partyplanningfun.co.uk – they'll have everything you need. Now I know you always say you have far too many clothes, but you must buy yourself a smashing new outfit – you are the star of the party after all!

I am terribly excited now! Let me know if you need any help or if you need me to bring along any music or party games (I have lots). I can't wait to see you!

All my love,

Jo xx

The writer uses **sobriquets** to refer to herself and the recipient.

Jo signs off with the words 'All my love'.

She concludes the letter by expressing her excitement and offering further help.

The writer outlines her advice. She makes a number of suggestions and justifies each one. She also uses **anecdotes** to support her recommendations.

The writer's address appears in the top right-hand corner.

42 Grove Road,
London

The recipient's address is also included in the letter.

Epicure Supermarket
Kingsbury
London

The writer is unfamiliar with the recipient so he uses **Sir/Madam** to address them.

Wednesday 17th February 2016

RE: Goods past their expiration date – chocolate biscuits
(Receipt No: 78933996)

A **subject line** is included to highlight the main issue to be addressed in the letter.

Dear Sir/Madam,

I am writing in order to complain about a pack of your own brand chocolate-covered biscuits, which I purchased from your store on Tuesday 16th February. These biscuits are well past their expiration date – June 2015 – and should not have been stocked on your shelves. I hope you will be able to exchange the item or offer me my money back.

The **purpose** for writing is immediately and clearly identified. The **main issue** or content is summarised briefly and the writer makes his **expectations** clear.

I have been a customer of yours for many years now and have always been satisfied with your service and the quality of your goods. However, last night, on reaching for a biscuit to accompany my cup of tea, I found that it was slightly green in colour. I assumed that it was merely food colouring so bit into it. It was only then that I realized that it was not food colouring but mould. I was absolutely horrified and am shocked that an organization of your scale could endanger their customers' health in such a way. I must confess that this has made me think twice about shopping at your store.

The writer describes the incident in greater detail, providing specific examples.

I hope that in future you will not be as careless, and I request that you exchange the item as soon as possible or offer me a full refund. I have attached to this letter a copy of my receipt and a photograph of the mouldy biscuit. Please do not hesitate to contact me if you require any further details.

I hope to hear from you soon.

Yours faithfully,

Mr J. Barrow

The writer concludes and reiterates his **expectations**. He has also included some additional details about what he has included with the letter.

The writer signs off with **'Yours faithfully'**.

---

5 What would life be like in a world without letters?

Persuasive writing

When was the last time you managed to convince someone to do something you wanted? Maybe you changed the way your best friend thinks about a certain pop song or video game? Perhaps you got your mum to let you stay up later than usual over the weekend?

Ask your friends if they've ever managed to change someone's mind about something or got someone to do something they hadn't planned on. In pairs or groups of three, **discuss** some of the techniques you used.

What have you come up with?

You might not realize it, but you've been using the art of **persuasion**! The purpose of **persuasion** is to get someone to change their viewpoint about a certain issue or to get someone to act in a way in which you want them to. For example, adverts successfully **persuade** us to buy things every day!

So, how can we be persuasive when we write? Here are some ideas:

- Address your audience by using **personal pronouns – I, you, we, us, our**. This engages your audience directly and can make them feel included and responsible. For example: *We all need to take part in the fight against climate change.*
- **Flatter** your audience and make them feel important. For example: *A **successful** company like yours understands the needs of its customers.*
- Make deals by using **conditional sentences** – this will make your audience feel that they have something to gain. For example: *If we use the bins provided, we **will** have a cleaner and more pleasant school environment.*
- Use **rhetorical questions** – these are questions that do not require an answer but are designed to make your audience or reader think. For example: *Can you imagine a world without war?*
- Make sure you provide justification and detailed support for your ideas. **Facts** and **statistics** can help show your reader that you know what you are talking about. For example: *71 per cent of the Earth's surface is water.*
- **Repetition** of certain words and phrases can be very effective as it makes your **message** more memorable. For example: In Martin Luther King's famous speech, he repeats the words *'I have a dream'* eight times.

EXTENSION: THE ETIQUETTE OF LETTER WRITING

Established in 1769, Debrett's is a publisher that specializes in the publication of guides on etiquette. Even today, Debrett's remains a trusted source on British social skills, etiquette and style.

Etiquette is usually a set of rules or customs that set out how one should behave in particular social situations. There is usually a great emphasis on politeness and propriety.

There are certain rules of etiquette that many people believe we should observe when writing letters.

Read the short text below taken from the Debrett's website and in pairs or groups of three, **discuss** the following:

- What attitudes and opinions are being expressed in the text?
- Why does the writer believe that writing letters is better than texting?
- Do you agree with the views that are expressed in the text?
- Choose a quote which you feel sums up the message of the text. Explain why you have chosen this example.

For more information about the etiquette of letter writing, visit the Debrett's website.

https://www.debretts.com/expertise/etiquette/correspondence/letters-and-cards/

www.debretts.com/british-etiquette/communication/written-etiquette/letters/general-rules

Art of letter writing

In our modern times, the art of letter writing should not be forgotten. The dangers of email, the bashed-out 'R U OK? I am gr8' ugliness of texting, the over-impulsive angry phone-call – all these fade into white noise beside the elegant, deliberated simplicity of a note written by hand.

Crisp vellum stationery, the elegant flow of letters pouring across a page: these are the building blocks of our civilisation.

Yes, we now have the printed word but do we want future civilisations to believe that ours was an age of bank statements and bureaucracy? Where are the love letters, the tellings-off from parent to errant teenager, the little billet-doux of correspondence that make the world go round? Stored on hard drives, listened to by bugging governments, deleted from voicemails?

Writing by hand focuses the mind. There is no delete button, no backspace, so words must be considered and chosen carefully before being committed to paper, making their meaning all the more succinct. Handwritten notes are both personal and permanent; a love letter is worth a thousand texts.

How can letters help bring us closer together?

For many of us, the most important reason for writing letters is to preserve and strengthen the bond we have with those we love and cherish the most. It's always great to know that someone out there is thinking of you, and what better way than through a letter?

Through letters we can gain a certain intimacy with those we are writing to. When we put pen to paper, we become consumed in thought about the receiver and the experiences we want to share with them. We also derive pleasure in the act of reading letters, as recipients ourselves, immersing ourselves in the words and worlds of our loved ones.

In the modern age, our existence is a global one. Over time, whether in the pursuit of new opportunities or for the sake of necessity, we have spread far and wide, across the world, and are often compelled to leave our friends and families behind. Through letters we can begin to build bridges back to these people who mean so much to us.

To the lonely, a simple letter from a friend or family member is a little ray of sunshine which can bring hope to their lives and comfort in the knowledge that someone out there is thinking of them.

We must make sure that our generation honours this incredibly important means of reaching out to others. It would be a terrible shame to let the art of letter writing die out and we should all play our part in keeping it alive.

! Take action

! Think about someone in your life who might be feeling lonely and brighten up their life by sending them a letter!

ACTIVITY: The lost art of letter writing

■ ATL

Critical-thinking skills: Revise understanding based on new information and evidence

Watch the video and listen to Lakshmi Pratury talk about why letters matter to her: www.ted.com/talks/lakshmi_pratury_on_letter_writing?language=en.

Answer the following questions:

1 **What legacy did Pratury's father leave behind for her?**
2 **What did this legacy make her realize?**
3 **What does she think about emails?**
4 **How does she use letters to remain connected to her loved ones?**

In pairs, or groups of three, **discuss** the following:
- **How do you think letters can help us connect with others?**
- **Do you agree with Pratury that letters should be able to co-exist with emails? Or does one come at the price of the other?**
- **Have you ever connected with someone through a letter?**

Think of a friend or family member you haven't been in touch with for a while. Use this opportunity to reconnect with them through writing a letter.

◆ Assessment opportunities

In this activity you have practised skills that are assessed using Criterion A: Listening and Criterion C: Speaking.

ℹ **legacy**: something left or handed down

Personification

You may have noticed that in the video, Pratury says that she saw her father's body 'being swallowed by fire'. She is referring to a religious Hindu custom of cremation on a funeral pyre. She brings the fire to life by using the verb 'swallowed'. This is an example of personification.

Personification is an effective literary technique used to give inanimate objects or concepts human characteristics. You can use personification to enrich your writing.

For example: *The tree **danced** in the wind.*

Here, to describe the movement of the tree, we have used the **verb 'danced'** – an action we are more likely to associate with people than objects.

Let's see if we can use personification to make the following sentence more interesting:

My phone rang.

Which verbs, that we would normally use to describe human sounds, could you use to replace the verb 'rang' in the sentence above? List as many as you can.

Here are two possible alternatives:

screeched   sang

Does changing the verb affect the meaning of the sentence at all? Consider 'My phone screeched' versus 'My phone sang'.

- Which of the two is more positive?
- What might the writer or character feel about their phone in each case?

Can you think of any other examples of personification?

WATCH–PAIR–SHARE

ATL

Reflection skills: Consider ethical, cultural and environmental implications

Critical-thinking: Identify trends and forecast possibilities

They say a picture is worth a thousand words, which perhaps explains why the greeting card industry is booming!

Every year millions are spent on buying cards for all sorts of occasions, whether it is to celebrate an annual festival or to apologize for something.

Cards are a wonderful way of showing someone that they are in your thoughts, especially if you don't have the time to write them a letter.

Watch this video entitled 'A Potted History of the Greeting Card': www.youtube.com/watch?v=XCMQ jyh0Jxs and consider the following questions:
- **What is the purpose of the video?**
- **Identify** how the creator of the video makes the video engaging.
- **Summarise** the most surprising or interesting thing you learnt from the video.

In pairs, or groups of three, complete tasks the following:
- **Evaluate** why people give each other greeting cards and for what purposes.
- Have you ever sent or received a greeting card?
- Do you prefer to write your own message or to use cards with a pre-printed message?
- **Identify** the conventions of a good card.
- **In your home country or as a part of your culture, is there a tradition of giving and receiving greeting cards?**
- **Will people continue to send postcards in the future? Why? Why not?**
- **Are there any occasions that you feel the greeting card industry has neglected? Can you think why? Do you think there is a need for greeting cards of this type?**
- **With this in mind, as an extension, design your own greeting card for one of these occasions.**

Assessment opportunities

In this activity you have practised skills that are assessed using Criterion A: Listening and Criterion C: Speaking.

ACTIVITY: Wish you were here!

ATL

Information literacy skills: Access information to be informed and inform others

Postcards are another fantastic way to send **messages** by post. The earliest known postcard dates from 1840 and was sent by a Londoner called Theodore Hook to … himself! Apparently he posted the card to his own address in Fulham, London, as a practical joke. The card was found in 2001 and was sold at auction for a remarkable £31,750!

Postcards differ from letters as they can be sent without envelopes. Just attach a stamp and an air-mail sticker and it's ready to post! Of course, this means that they are not as private, but this doesn't deter people from sending thousands each year!

Visit the link to access the multimodal text and complete the following tasks. **https://www.bbc.co.uk/ programmes/articles/srTWW4MSlYXbtNWN7kBMVD/ postcards-better-than-your-selfie.**

ACTIVITY: Writing postcards

ATL

Communication skills: Write for different purposes

Writing a postcard is a little bit like writing a short note. You don't have a great deal of space and, when abroad, you might not have much time, so just a few lines are usually enough. Keep your writing simple and don't be afraid to omit words to shorten your sentences – just be careful that they still make sense! For example, instead of writing 'I am having a lovely time', you could get away with 'Having a lovely time'.

Look at the example below.

The salutation or greeting. If you're stuck, here are some examples: *Hi Everyone; Greetings from sunny Spain; Wish you were here; Having the best time.*

The message is written on the left side of the card.

The address appears on the right side of the card. If you're sending it back home from abroad, don't forget to include the country!

Greetings from India!
Having a great time here in Jaipur. Hotel is lovely. Food and drink are super cheap!

Weather sometimes too hot for my liking. Lots of amazing things to see and do. Met some people from Canada. Going on an elephant ride tomorrow! Excited!

See you soon
Cristina

PS I've bought you the best gift ever!

Ben Thomas
22 Laurier Avenue
West Ottawa
Ontario,
Canada
K1B 0G5

The sign-off. Here are some suggestions: *Love (sender's name); See you soon; That's all the news for now; Best wishes; Lots of love.*

PS stands for postscript and is usually something you have forgotten to include in the main body of your letter or message. This is why it appears after the sign-off.

Answer the following questions:

1 **Identify** the factors that have contributed to the decline of postcard production in recent years?

2 What attitudes about postcards are expressed by the writer? How far do you agree with the writer's views?

3 Why were postcards more popular than letters?

4 How do the visual aspects of the text link to the written text? Consider the images and use of colour. **Explain** why you think the producers of this multimodal text have made these choices.

5 **Explain** why postcards are an important historical resource. Choose one of the images and **discuss** it with a partner or group. What makes it special? What does it reveal about life at the time the image was created?

Shall we have a go at writing our own postcard?

Look at the following entry taken from 11-year-old Faisal's journal. It is from a day he spent in Paris last autumn while on holiday with his family.

Synthesise the information and use it to write a message on a postcard to his best friend.

You should not write more than 100 words if you can help it!

Saturday 21st October 2015

10 am – Just arrived at the hotel. Mum checking us in while Dad panicking about where he's put our passports. I can't believe I have to share a room with Sara!

11:30 am – Waiting in the queue outside the Louvre. It seems never-ending. There's no way we're going to make it for lunch on time at that restaurant Mum booked.

2 pm – Lunch at Angelina. Having the thickest hot chocolate ever. It was worth waiting for the gallery – so many cool pictures. Had to fight through crowds of people to see the Mona Lisa. I thought it was great, but Mum must've found it sad because she cried. Aaaargh, Sara has just spilt her drink all over me!

4 pm – Notre Dame. Cathedral is a bit boring so I'm just having a sit down. Loved being up there with the gargoyles though. Kept hoping we'd catch sight of the hunchback! I want to go back to the gift shop so I can pick up some souvenirs.

6:30 pm – We're at the top of the Eiffel Tower, even though it's freezing! Dad waiting at the bottom – he's had enough of heights for one day. I can see for miles! Mum's telling me to put my journal away or it'll blow away in the wind.

9 pm – Stuffed from a dinner of moules frites – didn't think much of the moules part but the frites were yummy. In a cab on the way back to the hotel so a bit difficult to write. Sara fallen asleep with her head on my shoulder. Think I can feel her drool … yuck! Mum excited about going to some place called Versailles tomorrow.

How have letters influenced literature, art and culture?

Over the years, letters have become far more than just tools for communication. They have found their way into books, films and even popular songs! Letters can allow us to be creative in unexpected ways and can be a great way to share stories.

You may be surprised to learn that the earliest novels were written in the form of letters. A story that is told through letters is known as an **epistolary narrative**, and some of the greatest writers in history have used letters in their books. Sometimes a writer will include a letter to give us a different perspective or to allow us to get into the mind of a particular character.

Do you know of any stories that have been told using letters? Or any books that have contained letters? Can you think of any popular songs about letters from your country or culture?

Did you know that the term *epistolary* comes from the word *epistle*? An *epistle* is basically a form of writing directed to a person or group of people. While this usually means letters, *diaries* can also fall into this same category. After all, aren't diaries just letters to ourselves? Perhaps this is why so many of us begin our diary entries with the words 'Dear Diary'.

A great example is *The Diary of Anne Frank* – a diary kept by a young Jewish girl who was trying to flee persecution from the Nazis during the Second World War. In this remarkable account, the diary and letter forms collide – Anne didn't address her writing to her diary, but rather wrote letters to an imaginary friend called 'Kitty', with whom she shared her innermost thoughts and secrets.

Do you keep a diary?

ACTIVITY: *Heidi*

ATL

Communication skills: Read critically and for comprehension

Heidi is a novel written in 1881 by the Swiss author Johanna Spyri. It is one of the best-selling children's books ever written.

The story follows the events in the life of a young girl called Heidi and is set in Germany and the Swiss Alps. In the story, Heidi receives a letter from her friend Clara.

Read the extract and complete the following tasks. Make sure you use evidence from the text to support each response.

1 **Identify** the kind of letter this is.
2 **Identify** Clara's main purpose for writing.
3 **Identify** why they can't set out on their journey immediately.
4 Clara's father will be going with her to the mountains. Is this statement true or false?
5 **Summarise** the significant information we learn about Clara from her letters.
6 **Evaluate** how the doctor has changed and why.
7 **Identify** why Fraulein Rottenmeier doesn't want to go with them.
8 **Find** two contrasting descriptions of the mountains. **Analyse** how people perceive things in different ways.
9 Can you find an example of personification in the text? **Interpret** the effect of this.
10 What can you infer about the relationship between Clara and Heidi?

In pairs, **discuss** the following:
- **Do you think using letters is an effective way of driving a story forward?**
- **Discuss the advantages of using letters to tell a story.**

◆ Assessment opportunities

In this activity you have practised skills that are assessed using Criterion B: Reading.

The past continuous tense

Most stories are written or told in the past tense. In Chapter 3 page 61, we looked at the past simple tense. Look back to remind yourself about when we use the past simple.

The past continuous tense takes the following form:

was/were + present participle

The **present participle** of a verb is the simple form of the verb with an *ing* attached at the end. For example, the verb *think* becomes *thinking*.

The past continuous tense is used to describe an action or an event that was taking place in the past, at a certain point in time. We often use the past continuous tense to describe actions that take place while something else is happening at the same time.

For example: *Yesterday afternoon I was reading a novel while my dad cooked dinner.*

(past simple)   (past continuous)

Dearest Heidi,

Everything is packed and we shall start now in two or three days, as soon as papa himself is ready to leave; he is not coming with us as he has first to go to Paris. The doctor comes everyday, and as soon as he is inside the door, he cries, 'Off now as quickly as you can, off to the mountain.' He is most impatient about our going. You cannot think how much he enjoyed himself when he was with you! He has called nearly every day this winter, and each time he has come into to my room and said he must tell me about everything again. And then he sits down and describes all he did with you and the grandfather, and talks of the mountains and the flowers and of the great silence up there far far above all towns and the villages, and of the fresh delicious air, and often adds, 'No one can help getting well up there.' He himself is quite a different man since his visit, and looks quite young again and happy, which he had not been for a long time before. Oh, how I am looking forward to seeing everything and to being with you on the mountain and to making the acquaintance of Peter and the goats.

I shall have first to go through a six weeks' cure at Ragatz; this the doctor has ordered, and then we shall move up to Dorfli, and every fine day I shall be carried up the mountain in my chair and spend the day with you. Grandmamma is travelling with me and will remain with me; she also is delighted at the thought of paying you a visit. But just imagine, Fraulein Rottenmeier refuses to come with us. Almost every day grandmamma says to her, 'Well, how about this Swiss journey, my worthy Rottenmeier? Pray say if you really would like to come with us.' But she always thanks grandmamma very politely and says she has quite made up her mind. I think I know what has done it: Sebastian gave such a frightful description of the mountain, of how the rocks were so overhanging and dangerous that any minute you might fall into a crevasse, and how it was such steep climbing that you feared at every step to go slipping to the bottom, and that goats alone could make their way up without fear of being killed. She shuddered when she heard him tell of all this, and since then she has not been so enthusiastic about Switzerland as she was before. Fear has also taken possession of Tinette, and she also refuses to come. So grandmamma and I will be alone; Sebastian will go with us as far as Ragatz and then return here.

I can hardly bear waiting till I see you again. Good-bye, dearest Heidi; grandmamma sends you her best love and all good wishes.

Your affectionate friend,

Clara

ACTIVITY: Literary letters

ATL

Creative-thinking skills: Create original works and ideas; use existing works and ideas in new ways

The Letters about Literature project is an initiative in the USA designed to promote reading and writing. It is a competition that invites students aged between 9 and 18 to read a book, poem or play and write a letter to the author, living or dead, about how they have been personally affected by the text.

The competition is open to students residing in the USA, but that doesn't mean that we can't all have a go at writing to our favourite writers!

For more information, and some guidelines on how to get started, follow the link: **http://read.gov/documents/LAT15-Flyer2.pdf**.

In pairs or groups of three, discuss the last book, poem or play you read. Each of you may choose to give your group a short summary and explain what you liked about the text.

On your own:
- **Use a search engine to find out whether the author of your text is living or dead. Carry out some research about their life, interests and other achievements.**
- **If your author is living, check to see if they have their own website. You may be able to post your letter directly to them. Ask a parent or teacher to help you organize this. Who knows, if you're lucky, you may even get a response!**

Now, follow the Read, Reflect and Persuade guidelines in the link above and, bearing in mind what you have learnt about writing letters in this chapter, write a letter to the author telling them about how their work has affected you personally.

Before you begin to write:
- **Think about whether your letter should be formal or informal.**
- **Once you have decided, consider which conventions your letter should include.**
- **Plan your letter carefully. Don't forget to organize your writing using paragraphs. Think about what you want each paragraph to be about.**

◆ Assessment opportunities

In this activity you have practised skills that are assessed using Criterion C: Speaking and Criterion D: Writing.

EXTENSION: LETTERS LIVE

Letters Live is an event that celebrates and brings literary correspondence to life through performance and live readings. At each event, letters written by politicians, actors, writers, musicians and artists of the past are read aloud by their modern celebrity counterparts.

Follow the link below and check out just some of the letters that have been shared with audiences during past events.

http://letterslive.com/letters/

- What do we gain from sharing letters written by famous people from the past?
- Should letters be read aloud or do you think they should remain private?
- What techniques do the performers use to bring these letters to life?

What do letters reveal about the past?

CAN LETTERS BE USED AS WEAPONS?

The written word, whether it be in the form of official documents or literature, has always provided us with a window into history. Historians have learnt that it is through understanding individual histories, the experiences and emotions of everyday people, that we can construct a fuller and more accurate image of the past. These personal **narratives** can be found in the pages of letters written by men and women over time.

Through letters we can gain an insight into the impact that major historical events had on the lives of people. We can learn about day-to-day living, cultural practices, social attitudes and the collective and personal anxieties people harboured at the time of writing. There are, of course, some gaps – you need to be literate in order to write, so there are sadly some voices we will never hear first-hand through letters or stories.

Letters have also been the means of preserving important historical texts – words of wisdom that would otherwise have faded over time.

We have already explored the power of letters in this chapter but we must not forget the role that letters and letter writing have played in our development over the course of time. For a very long time letters were our only means of global communication – without them, trade, exploration and progress would never have been possible. Letters have been instrumental in bringing about social change through challenging people's ideas about themselves and the worlds to which they belong. Through reading and writing letters we can uncover great truths – about ourselves and our place in history.

■ Soldier writing a letter in the trenches

ACTIVITY: Letters to loved ones

During the First World War, the only way soldiers could keep in touch with their loved ones back at home was through exchanging letters. Many of these letters have survived and are an invaluable source of information about the lives of people during this testing time. These letters not only give us a snapshot of the conditions these young men had to endure on the front lines but also give us a glimpse into the lives of civilians during the war.

The Imperial War Museum in London holds around 7,500 collections of personal letters sent between 1914 and 1918 in their archives.

Follow the link to read some of these letters:
www.iwm.org.uk/history/letters-to-loved-ones.

Answer the following questions:

1 How many letters were exchanged during the war?
2 Why are the letters so valuable? Give at least two reasons.
3 Are the letters formal or informal? **Explain** why.
4 Which letter is your favourite? **Explain** why.
5 Re-read your favourite letter and copy and complete the table below:

	Answer	Evidence from text
What is the relationship between the writer and the recipient?		
What do you think the main purpose of the letter is?		
What do we learn about the impact of the war from this letter?		
How does this letter make you feel? Are there any particular words which evoke these feelings?		

6 Are there any new words you have come across in your chosen letter? Using a dictionary, compile a glossary of new words.

▼ Links to: Individuals and societies – History

Historians rely on all sorts of resources when they are studying the past. The written word is especially important for historical study, as we have already seen in this section, and letters are often used as primary sources.

Primary sources are documents or artefacts created during a particular period in history. Primary sources can include letters, diaries and photographs. They are important because they can reflect the individual perspective of a participant or observer at a certain point in time. Primary sources are valuable as they allow us to get really close to what happened in the past.

Of course, we have to be careful when we use primary sources – sometimes diaries and letters can provide us with a biased or one-sided viewpoint; they might not present information accurately; sometimes we need to ascertain whether the source is genuine or not before we can trust it.

ACTIVITY: Weapons of war?

Watch the short clip about letters sent during the First World War from the BBC, presented by Alan Johnson, who is an MP and former postman.
https://youtu.be/hYQ4h9_WNOM

After watching:

1 **Identify** why letters were so important for soldiers during the First World War.
2 **Explain** what you understand by the word 'censored'. Can you come up with a definition of your own?
3 Why were the soldiers' letters read by censors? What do you think about this?
4 **Evaluate** how you would feel if someone read your private letters.
5 **Summarize** what you have learnt about the role of letters during the First World War.
6 It has been said that the letter was one of the most powerful weapons of the First World War. **Interpret** what this might mean. How far do you agree with this statement?

Look carefully at the posters below. They date from the First and Second World Wars.

In pairs or groups of three, **discuss** both multimodal texts and for each one complete the following tasks. Make sure you find appropriate evidence to support your answers.

1 **Identify** the purpose of the multimodal text.
2 **Identify** the target audience.
3 **Analyse** the message that the creators of the visual text are trying to convey.
4 **Summarise** how the images help to convey the message and how they link to the text.
5 What kind of language is used to convey the message?
6 How do these visual texts link to:
   a the information and letters from the Imperial War Museum page
   b the short video from the BBC?
7 **Discuss** how these posters make you feel.

Is letter writing at risk of dying out?

HOW CAN WE REVIVE THE ART OF LETTER WRITING?

In an age when we're becoming increasingly dependent on computers and phones as our main tools for communication, is there still a place for letter writing? After all, who has the time to scribble away using such primitive tools as pens or pencils? What happens if you make a mistake or forget to include something? You have to cross it out and leave an ugly mark on your otherwise unblemished piece of paper or, worse still, start all over again! What an horrendous prospect! Much easier to send an email.

But aren't we losing something when we stop putting pen to paper? Is there anything really so wrong with taking time to think about the message we want to communicate, so that it can be put down perfectly, first time, without any need for modifications? There is something quite soothing about hearing the sound of a pencil scratching across the surface of a page or watching deep, blue ink seep into your paper. The written letter has a permanence that the email lacks. An email can be changed, deleted, reproduced, shared and much more. The letter, once it has been written and sent, can sit safely in the hands of the recipient and is there forever, until it is physically lost or wilfully discarded.

Perhaps there is room for the handwritten letter to exist side by side with the email; they do, after all, share a common goal. The introduction of a new form of correspondence doesn't necessarily mean that another should be compromised.

ⓘ Did you know that technology has always been a threat to the art of letter writing? In the nineteenth century people sent messages by **telegraph**. These messages were known as **telegrams**. For the first time in history, people could send short messages over long distances almost instantaneously. The cost of a telegram was determined by the number of words used. A telegram with a longer message cost more, while shorter messages obviously cost less. Because of this, telegrams were kept short and to the point.

ACTIVITY: A Technology Society

■ ATL

Communication skills: Use a variety of speaking techniques to communicate with a variety of audiences; take effective notes in class

Critical-thinking skills: Evaluate evidence and arguments

Task 1

A Technology Society (www.atechnologysociety.co.uk) is a society dedicated to providing readers with valuable and up-to-date information and advice on technology. Writers who claim to be experts in the field regularly post blogs and articles evaluating the effect that technology has had on society.

Read the article by Chris Nickson on page 120, which is taken from the Technology Society website.

Make some notes about the article, with the following questions in mind:

1 **What appear to be the disadvantages of letter writing?**
2 **Who in society is more likely to want to continue the tradition of letter writing?**
3 **According to the writer, what are the benefits of email?**

What is a debate?

A **debate** is a structured **argument** between two sides or parties about a topical issue. A debate isn't like an argument you might have with family or friends – each side has to take turns to present their arguments, which are then challenged by the opponent.

In a debate, it is useful to have an understanding of the other side of the argument. This shows that you can be balanced and objective and will also give you a better idea of what the other side might use to attack your arguments.

But remember, you need to get your argument across in order to win, so make sure that you present your ideas as **clearly** and as **logically** as possible, preferably with lots of facts and supporting details to help justify them.

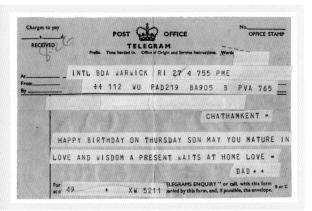

If you need a reminder on how to take effective notes, refer back to page 53 in Chapter 3.

Task 2

So, is it time we accepted the idea that there will be no room in the future for letters and that emails are the way forward when it comes to correspondence? Or should we fight to keep the art of letter writing alive?

Let's have a debate!

Split into two groups.

In your groups, copy and complete the table below. You can use information you have come across earlier in this chapter or use the internet to carry out some further research. Make sure you can **justify** and support all of your arguments.

Decide on which group is going to present the argument for preserving the art of letter writing and which group is going to present the argument that emails are the future.

Ready, steady … debate!

Let the best form of correspondence win!

Task 3

Things have moved on again since this article was written. Consider the following questions:

1 **Do you agree with Nickson that email is one of the main ways we use to communicate in today's world? If not, explain why.**
2 **How do people your age communicate today? Are computers being displaced by mobile phones?**

What are the advantages of letter writing?	What are the disadvantages of letter writing?	What are the advantages of emails?	What are the disadvantages of emails?

 Assessment opportunities

In this activity you have practised skills that are assessed using Criterion B: Reading and Criterion C: Speaking.

Has email replaced letter writing?

Email. We use it daily, check it regularly – some people check it obsessively. On a computer, on a smartphone like a BlackBerry or iPhone, it's one of the main ways we communicate with other people.

Now computers are so prevalent we use them to send documents, music, even pictures and videos, all attached to a short email note. Where we once wrote letters, now we drop people an email. But is it the same thing, just in a different form? No, it's not.

How email took over from letter writing

It takes a while to write a letter. You sit down with a blank sheet of paper and pour out your news – usually several weeks' worth (if it's a personal rather than a business letter, of course) since the last letter.

Letter writing is an art, sometimes boring, sometimes exciting, but full of detail. For several centuries it was the main way people stayed in touch, especially those who'd moved elsewhere, whether to other parts of the country or abroad.

Letter writing was a process that could take an hour or several days, depending on the length of the epistle. Letters were joyfully received and replies penned. They were saved and treasured and often handed down through families as keepsakes and histories.

The transition to email wasn't instant. It couldn't be – only as computers became widespread could it become the prevalent medium. Of course, there are still plenty of people who prefer words on paper, especially among the older generation, but in a society that's come to value instant gratification, the appeal of email – write it, click a button and it zips off to the recipient – makes a lot of sense.

These days most people communicate by email. Asking for someone's address means their email address, not house number and street name (it goes right along with the mobile number). The email address – and many people have several, including a number of easily portable web-based mail addresses – is printed on our business cards.

Email means we're in touch. You can check it on the road, from another country and reply – there's no waiting until you're home and seeing what the postman's left. You can even email from your phone if it's important.

The difference between letters and email

Personal letters were long things, but when was the last time you received a long, rambling email? They're very rare. Instead they tend to be short notes with a brief bit of news, knocked off very quickly, often as we're in the middle of several other things. They've changed the art of letter writing. How many people would want to save emails? Some are worthwhile, but they're few and far between.

Now, instead of going into depth, the way we did in letters, we skim the surface of things in order to finish and move on quickly. If we want to include details, we attach a picture or even a video. We communicate by email, but we rarely talk. Replies to questions are generally brief. Compared to letters, emails are little more than an exchange of notes – and for the most part, letter writing has fallen by the wayside.

Emails and business letters

Personal letter writing is one thing, business letters are another. They're ideally suited to the email format, being more formal and short. There's no rambling, simply addressing the points involved.

All email has done for business letters, really, is speed up the process, and made things easier by allowing documents and files to be attached, so business – especially global business – runs more efficiently. In that regard it's been a boon – no more waiting several days for an airmail letter containing important contracts to arrive; they can speed to the other side of the world in seconds.

Chris Nickson

Take action: How can I make a difference?

! We can all do our bit to help keep the art of letter writing alive. Here are some fun ways in which you can make a difference …

- ◆ Become a pen-pal! A pen-pal or pen-friend is a person who you develop a friendship with through exchanging letters. Many people write to their pen-pals for years and years without ever meeting! It can be a great way to learn about another culture. To find yourself a pen-pal, approach a teacher – perhaps they can put you in touch with kids from a school in another country. Or why not ask your parents? They might have contacts somewhere who have children of a similar age to you.

- ◆ Start your own letter-writing club! Invite your friends at school to pair up with someone and write letters to each other regularly.

- ◆ Haven't heard from your grandma in a while? Or perhaps there's a friend out there you haven't spoken to in ages? Surprise them with a lovely handwritten letter!

- ◆ Why not write an open letter for your school magazine or blog? Unlike most letters, an **open letter** is not addressed to one person but rather a group of people. It doesn't have to be too personal, but can be a good way to express your feelings or share your ideas about an issue that is important to you. You might want to write an open letter to the students at your school to encourage them to use the bins instead of littering. See if you can come up with some other ideas.

- ◆ Make a pledge to send at least one postcard to a friend or family member when you are next on holiday.

SOME SUMMATIVE TASKS TO TRY

Use these tasks to apply and extend your learning in this chapter. These tasks are designed so that you can evaluate your learning in the Language acquisition criteria.

THIS TASK CAN BE USED TO EVALUATE YOUR LEARNING IN CRITERION B AT PROFICIENT LEVEL

Task 1: Dear pen pal: reading comprehension

- Use your own words as much as possible.
- Do not use translating devices or dictionaries for this task.
- You will have 60 minutes to complete this task.

Read the following article from *The Guardian* online and answer the questions that follow.

1 **Identify** when Margaret began to write letters. (strand i)

2 **Identify** what she didn't do as a child which prompted her to write. (strand i)

3 In paragraph three, what do 'Pen pal enthusiasts' say about handwriting? (strand ii)

4 In the context of the article, what does the word *enduring* mean? Choose one of the following:
   a to put up with something
   b long lasting
   c temporary
   d pleasant. (strand ii)

5 Which adjective in the first paragraph of the article suggests that writing letters was once an important part of childhood? (strand ii)

6 Zoe refuses to use technology and insists on handwriting everything. Is this statement true or false? Support your answer with evidence from the text. (strand ii)

7 **Analyse** how Sami's personality has changed since she began exchanging letters. **Interpret** and support your answer with two examples from the text. (strand i)

8 a Find a word in the text which means 'to write in a hurried or careless way'.
   b **Comment** on the effect the writer achieves by using this verb. (strand i)

9 Find an example of personification in the second paragraph. What is the effect of this? (strand ii)

10 Sami says 'There's a coldness with email that I find a handwritten letter doesn't possess – it's like opening a hug'. **Interpret** what she means by this. In your answer, explain the effect of the simile she uses. (strand ii)

11 How does the writer use the layout of the web page to make the text more accessible? (strand iii)

12 Do you agree with what Sami says? Do you think letters are better than emails? Explain why. (strand iii)

13 **Summarize** the message the writer is trying to convey. Support your answer with evidence from the text. (strand iii)

14 Based on your reading of this text, **evaluate** what can be gained through exchanging handwritten letters. Support your answer using evidence from the text. (strand iii)

www.theguardian.com/lifeandstyle/2014

Dear pen pal: how writing letters to strangers is making a comeback

You might assume email and social media had killed off the traditional pen pal, but simple letter writing has an enduring appeal, as three sets of correspondents testify

For many of us, pen pals were a staple part of childhood. Schools, Guides and Scouts groups regularly paired up overseas buddies, promoting cultural exchange and helping with language practice. Scrawled notes detailing favourite hobbies and pets' names were sent back and forth and, while most correspondences fizzled out after the first couple of letters, some continued for many years.

It would be easy to assume that email and social media killed off the traditional pen pal. However, it seems the hobby is undergoing a revival. Online schemes such as the International Geek Girl Pen Pals Club and The League of Extraordinary Pen Pals are springing up, connecting letter writers around the world. Projects such as indie lifestyle mag Oh Comely's care packages encourage strangers to send beautifully prepared, intricate parcels to one another. Even Reddit has its own pen pal sub-forum.

There is more to the trend than simple analogue festishisation. Pen pal enthusiasts (who, interestingly, seem to be mostly women) say they find handwriting relaxing and meditative, and believe their written relationships are just as central to their lives as face-to-face ones. We spoke to three sets of women about what inspired them to put pen to paper, and the role their friendships have played in their lives.

Margaret and Ingrid

Margaret Roberts, now 68, began writing to pen pals in her early teens. 'I didn't travel as a child, so having friends in other countries was a window to the world,' she recalls. At the age of 11, she answered a call-out for pen pals placed by a Swedish schoolteacher in her local paper, the Liverpool Echo. The result was a written friendship with Ingrid Andersson, now 70, which has lasted 57 years.

Throughout this time the pair have experienced a similar succession of life events. 'We had children at the same time; met partners at the same time, and even went through losing our parents together,' she explains. The women also followed near-identical career paths, both working as careers advisers. 'It's almost as if we've lived parallel lives,' says Margaret. 'It means we always have lots to talk about.'

They have met face-to-face on several occasions, and have both developed strong interests in each other's countries – Margaret even makes the effort to attend Scandinavian Santa Lucia festivals in the UK. And, as a bonus, Ingrid reports the friendship has hugely improved her English.

Zoe and Megan

The world of social media provided a catalyst for an analogue friendship between Londoner Zoe Bateman, 27, and Californian Megan, 23. 'She commented on my blog and then I ordered an embroidered quote from her Etsy shop, which turned into a package swap,' explains Zoe. 'It continued from there. She's a fan of British culture and I love Americana, so we did a "country swap", sending local postcards, souvenirs and sweets.'

The pair regularly send each other trinkets, gifts and letters, and go to great lengths to create beautifully wrapped packages. 'It's such a joy to include little odds and ends to make it special, such as art work or stickers, so it can brighten up their day,' says Megan. Both also enjoy the process of handwriting. 'I find it relaxing – it's nice to take a break from everything tech-based and get out my stationery,' says Zoe. 'I never handwrite anything else.'

Zoe is hoping to meet Megan for the first time when she travels to the US next year. 'It feels a bit like a first date,' she laughs. 'It's a different type of friendship to seeing each other every day, but it still feels just as real.'

Arielle and Sami

Pen pal projects can also act as a link between those with niche interests. 'I [used to be a] really lonely person,' explains Sami Levett, 26, from Sydney, Australia. 'I had friends, but not many who gamed, read comics or liked sci fi.'

Sami discovered the International Geek Girls Pen Pal Club through Twitter, and immediately signed up. The project matches women from around the world according to their interests, and Sami was just as attracted to the idea of letter writing as she was to meeting like-minded people. 'There's a coldness with email that I find a handwritten letter doesn't possess – it's like opening a hug,' she elaborates.

Thanks to the project, Sami is now part of a group of seven women from Australia and North America who speak online daily as well as send letters and packages to each other. 'It gave me the courage to be my true self and not be ashamed of it,' she concludes. 'I wouldn't have the confidence I do now if it wasn't for those girls.'

Sami is hoping to visit one of the women, Arielle, 27, in Houston, Texas, later this year. 'One of the best things about penpalling is learning about different cultures,' says Arielle. 'So Sami's going to come over and experience a proper American Thanksgiving with us.'

Task 2: Writing letters

- Use your own words as much as possible.
- Do not use translating devices or dictionaries for this task.
- You will have 60 minutes to complete this task.

Follow the link below and look at the poster. It dates from the 1930s.
What do you think the purpose of this multimodal text might have been?

https://www.loc.gov/resource/cph.3b48755/

Over the years and across the world, various organisations have come up
with initiatives to encourage people to write letters. In September 2015,
Royal Mail, the biggest postal delivery company in the United Kingdom,
launched National Letter Writing Week, specifically targeting young
people.

Write a letter to your headteacher or principal persuading them to allow
your school to take part in this year's celebrations.

In your letter you may want to:
- **explain** why you think it is important for young people to write letters.
- make some suggestions about how your school can be involved.

Take some time to plan carefully before you begin to write. Remember to
use the appropriate conventions for your letter.

You should write between 300 and 400 words.

Reflection

In this chapter we have identified the **conventions** of letter writing, and seen how the way we write must be adapted for different **audiences** and **purposes**. In addition we have explored the importance of the letter as a tool for **communication** and celebrated its value as a means for preserving history, culture and **relationships**. Lastly, we have considered the place of letter writing in the modern world and have tried to revive this dying art.

Use this table to reflect on your own learning in this chapter.						
Questions we asked	Answers we found	Any further questions now?				
Factual: Why do we write letters? What makes a good letter?						
Conceptual: How can letters help bring us closer together? What do letters reveal about the past? How have letters influenced literature, art and culture? Why are letters important?						
Debatable: In an age of digital communication, is the art of letter writing at risk of dying out?						
Approaches to learning you used in this chapter:	Description – what new skills did you learn?	How well did you master the skills?				
		Novice	Learner	Practitioner	Expert	
Communication skills						
Collaboration skills						
Reflection skills						
Information literacy skills						
Critical-thinking skills						
Creative-thinking skills						
Learner profile attribute(s)	Reflect on the importance of being a communicator for your learning in this chapter.					
Communicator						

6 What is poetry?

Poetry is a uniquely **creative** form of **personal and cultural expression** that leaves much room for an **audience** to interpret meaning.

CONSIDER THESE QUESTIONS:

Factual: What is a poem? What are the conventions of a poem?

Conceptual: Why do we write poetry? How can we use poetry to express our thoughts, feelings and ideas? Does the way in which we share and write poems vary from place to place? How can we use poems to tell stories?

Debatable: Why does poetry matter? Should we still read poetry today? To what extent do words empower us? How does poetry mirror what it means to be human?

Now **share and compare** your thoughts and ideas with your partner, or with the whole class.

IN THIS CHAPTER WE WILL ...

■ **Find out** what poetry is and how to write our own poems.

■ **Explore** how we can use poetry as a way to express ourselves.

■ **Take action** to demonstrate how poetry is as relevant as ever in today's world.

'Every time you listen to another person reading out a poem, in school or on a stage or in a studio, every time you read a poem aloud to yourself or in the presence of others, you are also reading it into yourself and them. Voice helps to carry words farther and deeper than eye. These recordings maintain a tradition of oral performance that is as old as the art of poetry itself.' – Seamus Heaney on Poetry and Performance

■ Percy Shelley's poems are some of the most celebrated in English literature

■ These Approaches to Learning (ATL) skills will be useful …

- Communication skills
- Reflection skills
- Critical-thinking skills
- Creative-thinking skills
- Transfer skills

● We will reflect on this learner profile attribute …

- **Knowledgeable** – we develop and use conceptual understanding, exploring knowledge across a range of disciplines.

◆ Assessment opportunities in this chapter:

- **Criterion A**: Listening
- **Criterion B**: Reading
- **Criterion C**: Speaking
- **Criterion D**: Writing

THINK–PAIR–SHARE

Read the short text below. In pairs, **discuss** whether you notice anything unusual about it. Is anything missing? Share your ideas with the class.

> When people call this beast to mind they marvel more and more at such a little tail behind so large a trunk before

It's actually a poem called 'The Elephant', by Hilaire Belloc from *The Bad Child's Book of Beasts*. Have a go at turning it back into a poem! Think about where you might need to start a new line or where there should be a comma or full stop.

Hint
Use the words that rhyme to help you.

KEY WORDS

imagery	rhythm
poem	syllables
poetry	verse
rhyme	

Why does poetry matter?

Some historians believe that we began to create poetry before we even learnt how to write! Poetry has always been a part of our story and it has evolved over time to adapt to our changing lifestyles, attitudes and relationships. Poetry is all around us in some shape or form – from a jingle in a television commercial or a pop song playing on the radio, to the epic poetry produced by the ancient Greeks or the beautiful verses written by literary giants such as Keats or Shelley – and we just can't seem to get enough of it.

Poetry enriches our lives, teaches us empathy and compassion for others and helps us to express ourselves through language and imagery. Poetry doesn't impose the same restrictions as other forms of writing do, and has a certain music to it that cannot be found in the lines of a letter or a story. Through poetry, we can set ourselves free and open our minds to new possibilities. Poems can help us cross boundaries – they can be found in all cultures, and our shared love of verse can help us make connections with others.

For centuries philosophers and writers have contemplated what makes a poem a poem and whether we can truly tell a good poem from a bad one. Many people believe that poetry is essential to our lives, and without it life would be a little less magical.

In this chapter we will explore the world of poetry and see for ourselves all that it has to offer.

ACTIVITY: Poets on poetry – What's the big deal?

■ ATL

Communication skills: Negotiate ideas and knowledge with peers and teachers

So, what exactly is poetry and why all the fuss? Let's hear it from the poets themselves.

In pairs, **discuss** the following quotes from some famous poets. Complete the following:
- **Interpret** what each quote means.
- **Analyse** the thoughts, feelings, ideas or attitudes about poetry that are being expressed in these quotes.
- Which one do you like the most? **Explain** why.

'Poetry is when an emotion has found its thought and the thought has found words.' – Robert Frost

'Poetry is the spontaneous overflow of powerful feelings: it takes its origin from emotion recollected in tranquility.' – William Wordsworth

'If I read a book and it makes my whole body so cold no fire can ever warm me, I know that is poetry.' – Emily Dickinson

What do you think poetry is? What does poetry mean to you?

Write a 200-word paragraph **explaining** what you think a poem is.

◆ Assessment opportunities

In this activity you have practised skills that are assessed using Criterion B: Reading and Criterion D: Writing.

What is a poem?

Rules, rules and more rules! When it comes to writing, there always seem to be so many rules that we have to follow. While this also applies to the writing of poems, over the years many writers have chosen to abandon some of the common **conventions** of poetry, which means that defining a poem is harder than ever. However, as a new and aspiring poet, it's a good idea for you to pay attention to some of these basic rules to help you get started. To begin, we must first decide on what a poem actually is.

Most of the writing you have done over the course of this book falls into the category of **prose**, meaning that it follows the standard rules of **grammar** and appears in a certain way on the page. Poems, however, don't need to abide as strictly to these rules and we are given more freedom to play with **language**, **syntax** and **layout**. While most prose is written to be read, poems are written to be recited, so often, but not always, they have a certain **rhythm** and **rhyme** that other forms of writing may not have.

A poem is a type of literary text that allows writers to express themselves through making distinctive stylistic choices. Poetry has the power to convey feelings and ideas through language and imagery.

ACTIVITY: Poetry or prose?

■ ATL

Communication skills: Preview and skim texts to build understanding

Look at the extracts below. In groups of three, decide which ones you think are poetry and which are prose, and copy and complete the table below.

Make sure you can justify your choices!

'Between my finger and my thumb
The squat pen rests; as snug as a gun'

'There's no point crying over spilt milk'

'Blackout Britain'

'It was a bright cold day in April, and the clocks were striking thirteen.'

'The owl and the pussy-cat went to sea
In a beautiful pea-green boat,'

'Elvis Presley's teeth visit Malvern'

'Let sleeping dogs lie'

'The past is a foreign country: they do things differently there.'

'And when wind and winter harden
All the loveless land,
It will whisper of the garden,
You will understand'

Text type	Extract	Justification
Poem		
Newspaper headline		
Idiom		
Novel opening		

Still unsure about some of them? Use a search engine to find out which ones are from poems.

- **Which of the poetry extracts did you like the most?**
- **Identify the words or phrases that you found particularly interesting.**
- **Identify the techniques used by the writers.**

◆ Assessment opportunities

In this activity you have practised skills that are assessed using Criterion C: Speaking and Criterion B: Reading.

WHAT MAKES A POEM?

The following poem was written by the American poet Emily Dickinson in 1862. Dickinson didn't give many of her poems titles, so today we know it simply as poem number 632.

The poem is made up of three **stanzas**.

Let's take a look at what Dickinson has included in her poem.

■ Emily Dickinson wrote thousands of poems, but only a few were published in her lifetime

Have you ever been told off by a teacher for repeating yourself too much when you're writing? Well, you can get away with it in poetry! In fact, **repetition** is a technique that many writers use to create specific effects – repetition can be used to emphasize a key point that you want your **audience** to grasp or remember. It's not just words that can be repeated, but also grammatical structures. What things does Dickinson repeat and for what effect?

Notice how when you say these words, their endings make a similar sound. This is called a **rhyme**. Think about your favourite songs – don't most of them have **rhyming** words? **Rhymes** commonly appear at the end of lines – these can be lines that come directly one after the other or, as in this case, alternately (meaning the rhyme skips a line). Don't be fooled though – although many poems contain rhymes, there are plenty of others that don't!

As you read the poem, you will find that your mind will begin to conjure certain images or pictures. No, you're not going mad – it's because Dickinson uses language to create **imagery**. In this poem we have imagery of the sea, the sky, sponges and buckets and the brain.

> The brain—is wider than the sky—
> For—put them side by **side**
> The one the other will contain
> With ease—and you—**beside**
>
> The brain is deeper than the sea—
> For—hold them—blue to Blue—
> The one the other will absorb—
> **As sponges—buckets—do—**
>
> The brain is just the weight of God—
> For—heft them—pound for pound—
> And they will differ—if they do—
> As syllable from sound—

Dickinson makes certain **stylistic choices** to convey her **message**. Here she has used a **simile**, a literary technique that you have already encountered in Chapter 3. Refresh your memory by turning to page 62.

You may have noticed all the dashes (—) that appear in between some of the words and the lines in the poem. In poems, dashes and other punctuation marks can be used to show a **pause**. Remember, poems are written to be read aloud, so knowing when to pause can be useful for a reader and can help them control the **pace** at which they read. Pauses can also be included to add **dramatic effect** and give the audience a moment to reflect on the content they have just encountered. We don't know if these dashes were put in by Emily Dickinson herself, or whether it was done by her editors when they published her poems.

ACTIVITY: So, what makes a poem?

■ ATL

Communication skills: Make inferences and draw conclusions

Read the poem by Emily Dickinson on page 130 and complete the following tasks:

1 **Evaluate** how the poem looks different on the page from some of the other types of writing you have produced.
2 If you had to give the poem a title, what would it be and why?
3 **Interpret** the message of Dickinson's poem.
4 Create some similes of your own about your brain.

◆ Assessment opportunities

In this activity you have practised skills that are assessed using Criterion B: Reading.

Understanding stanzas

In **prose** we use **paragraphs** to arrange our writing, but in poems we use **stanzas**. A stanza can also be referred to as a **verse**.

A stanza is made up of a number of **lines** and is usually separated from the other stanzas in the poem by using a space. The number of lines in a stanza can vary; sometimes all the stanzas in a single poem contain the same number of lines but this is not always the case.

A poet can decide how many stanzas to include in their poem, and it is common to find poems that are written in a single stanza.

ACTIVITY: Spot the simile

■ ATL

Communication skills: Read critically and for comprehension

'The Warm and the Cold' is a poem written by Ted Hughes, an English poet and children's writer. Hughes grew up in Yorkshire and was deeply inspired by the rural landscape. He loved animals and many of his poems focus on the natural world.

Read the poem on page 132 and complete the following tasks:

1 How many similes can you spot in the poem?
2 **Evaluate** how Hughes uses similes to present the weather. **Interpret** the effect of these similes. How do they make you feel?
3 **Identify** how the animals in the poem cope with the winter. Choose one simile that illustrates this.
4 Look at the simile 'Like oxen on spits'. Who does it refer to and what is the effect?
5 **Analyse** the message of the poem. What point is Hughes making about humans and nature?

◆ Assessment opportunities

In this activity you have practised skills that are assessed using Criterion B: Reading.

The Warm and the Cold

Freezing dusk is closing
Like a slow trap of steel
On trees and roads and hills and all
That can no longer feel.
But the carp is in its depth
Like a planet in its heaven.
And the badger in its bedding
Like a loaf in the oven.
And the butterfly in its mummy
Like a viol in its case.
And the owl in its feathers
Like a doll in its lace.

Freezing dusk has tightened
Like a nut screwed tight
On the starry aeroplane
Of the soaring night.
But the trout is in its hole
Like a chuckle in a sleeper.
The hare strays down the highway
Like a root going deeper.
The snail is dry in the outhouse
Like a seed in a sunflower.
The owl is pale on the gatepost
Like a clock on its tower.

Moonlight freezes the shaggy world
Like a mammoth of ice –
The past and the future
Are the jaws of a steel vice.
But the cod is in the tide-rip
Like a key in a purse.
The deer are on the bare-blown hill
Like smiles on a nurse.
The flies are behind the plaster
Like the lost score of a jig.
Sparrows are in the ivy-clump
Like money in a pig.

Such a frost
The flimsy moon
Has lost her wits.

A star falls.

The sweating farmers
Turn in their sleep
Like oxen on spits.

Ted Hughes

■ Edgar Allan Poe uses sound in 'The Raven' to create an atmosphere of unease. It is believed that the poem was inspired by Charles Dickens's pet raven, Grip!

ℹ Did you know that Ted Hughes was the **Poet Laureate** of the United Kingdom from 1984 until his death in 1998? The post of Poet Laureate is a special honour awarded to a prominent poet by the government or the monarchy. The poet laureate is responsible for writing poetry for special occasions and major national events.

The current Poet Laureate for the United Kingdom is Simon Armitage, who was appointed in 2019.

Does your country have a celebrated poet? Are they referred to as Poet Laureate or do they they have a different title? If so, are you familiar with any of their work? Carry out some research to find out a little bit about them.

Share what you learn with your class.

The Elmet Trust
The birthplace of
Ted Hughes O M
1930 - 1998
Poet Laureate
Lived here 1930 - 1938
Calderdale Council   Halifax plc   Yorkshire Forward

■ Founded in 1866 and now run by English Heritage, the blue plaques link the people of the past with the buildings of the present

Sound in poetry

One of the most effective ways of bringing your writing to life or transporting your reader into the world of your poem, is by introducing sounds!

The easiest and (by far the most fun) is through the use of **onomatopoeia**. Onomatopoeia refers to words which create sounds, for example:

buzz   splash   hiss   pop   sizzle
whoosh   bang

Another simple way to introduce sound in your writing is through the use of **alliteration**. Alliteration is the repetition of sounds in a sentence or a line. For example, let's look at an extract from a poem by Edgar Allan Poe called 'The Raven'.

In the poem, the narrator is home alone on a dark winter's night and feeling a little jumpy because of someone constantly knocking on his door. Creepy, right? Every little noise becomes amplified and here he describes the sound of the curtains moving in the wind:

> 'And the silken, sad, uncertain rustling of each purple curtain
>
> Thrilled me – filled me with fantastic terrors never felt before;'

Which sound is being repeated? What effect does this create? Clever, isn't it?

Be careful! – some people mistakenly think that alliteration is the repetition of *letters* – this is wrong, as Poe's poem proves. More than one letter is capable of making a certain sound (**g**iraffe and **j**am; **c**ake and **k**ite; **s**eal and **c**eiling; **ph**one and **f**ish).

Can you find any examples of onomatopoeia or alliteration in the poems we have looked at in this chapter?

EXTENSION: LIST POEMS

 ATL

Communication skills: Give and receive meaningful feedback

Reflection skills: (Re)considering the process of learning; choosing and using ATL skills

Are you itching to write a poem of your own? **List poems** are a fantastic way to ease yourself into the writing process.

So, what is a list poem? A list poem does exactly what it says on the tin! It is quite simply a poem made up of a long list of things.

Let's take a look at an example written in 1940 by Jack Prelutsky, an American writer of children's poetry.

Find and read the poem, Bleezer's Ice Cream.

As you read the poem, consider the following:

1 How many stanzas are there in this poem?

2 **Evaluate** why a list poem might appeal to a younger audience.

3 How does the writer 'frame' his list?

4 How 'delicious' does the ice cream in Bleezer's freezer sound to you? Which words or phrases can you **identify** that contradict this point?

5 Can you **identify** a rhyme scheme? What is the effect of this?

Ready to have a go at writing your own poem?

Using Prelutsky's poem as a guide, write your own list poem about one of the following:
- adolescence
- computer games
- parents
- food.

Try to include some of the techniques we have explored already in this chapter.

Once you have written your poem, share it with a partner or in a group and give each other constructive feedback. Improve your poems with the feedback you have received.

◆ Assessment opportunities

In this activity you have practised skills that are assessed using Criterion B: Reading and Criterion D: Writing.

Why do we write poetry?

Did you know that in Greek mythology, there are nine goddesses of inspiration? They were known as **The Muses**, and each one presided over a particular branch of the arts – at least four of them were said to inspire poetry of various kinds.

In modern English, we use the term muse to refer to a person who inspires an artist, writer or musician.

One famous example is the poet and painter, Dante Gabriel Rossetti's muse, Elizabeth Siddal. In fact her distinctive beauty didn't just inspire Rossetti, but many of his contemporaries in the Pre-Raphaelite movement during the mid-nineteenth century, and her face can be found gazing out from many paintings of the period.

Rossetti was hopelessly in love with his muse, and when she died he placed a notebook of poetry in her grave to be buried with her. Isn't that romantic? Sadly, and rather disturbingly, seven years later, when Rossetti realized that his poetry could sell as well as his paintings, he exhumed her body and retrieved the notebook so the poems could be published! Not so romantic after all!

We are all different, so it is only natural that we should write poetry for different reasons. In the past, poetry was used to record important historical events or to share stories. For some writers, poems are a vehicle through which they can raise awareness about important universal issues and perhaps influence change; for others, poetry is a means for exploring personal identity or for making connections with others; some poets use poetry as a tool through which they can make sense of the world they live in and respond to their surroundings. The one thing they all have in common is their ability to recognize the power of poetry.

The list of things that inspire us to write poetry is as vast and as varied as the many reasons for writing it. We can be inspired by an internal thought, feeling or sensation or by something we have seen, read, heard, smelt, tasted or experienced. Sometimes we are inspired by people and at other times by places. Inspiration is all around us and we are limited only by our own imagination.

In this section not only will we look at the kind of things that have inspired some of the world's greatest poets, but will also find sources of inspiration to feed *your* imagination so that you can produce a poem or two of your own!

What inspires you? Create a mind map! Share your ideas in pairs or groups of three.

■ The nine muses show off their collective talents while Pegasus, the winged horse, hovers in the background

■ The beautiful Elizabeth Siddal – the face that inspired Rossetti's masterpieces of Pre-Raphaelite art

SEE–THINK–WONDER

Literature and art have always complemented one another. Artists including Waterhouse and Millais both have produced paintings inspired by the work of poets such as Tennyson, Keats and Shakespeare. However, this also works the other way around, and paintings can be an equally good source of inspiration for writing poetry.

Follow the link below to read some poems which have been inspired by paintings.

www.theartsdesk.com/visual-arts/listed-poems-inspired-paintings

1 Select your favourite poem inspired by a painting.
2 **Explain** what links there are between the poem and the painting.
3 **Identify** any stylistic choices the writer has made.
4 In your opinion, which is the best line in the poem? **Justify** your choice.

In pairs, look at the paintings and use the routine 'I see …, I think …, I wonder ….' and **discuss** the images. Make sure you backup your interpretation with reasons.

Choose **one** of the paintings below, and write a short poem inspired by what you see. Don't tell your partner or group which painting you've chosen.

What do you see? What do you think about it? What does it make you wonder?

Read over your poem and check that you've addressed the following:
- **Have you organized your poem using stanzas?**
- **Have you included any stylistic features (similes; personification; onomatopoeia; alliteration)?**
- **Does your poem rhyme?**

Share your poem with your partner or group by reading it aloud. See if they can guess which painting you were inspired by!

WHAT INSPIRED THE ROMANTICS?

Romanticism is a term that modern critics apply to an aesthetic movement that sprang up in the early nineteenth century. **The Romantics** were a group of artists, writers and thinkers who reacted against the rational ideas and classicism of the previous age; instead they found beauty in the unconventional, and marvelled at the unrestrained wildness of nature. The Romantics were inspired by their surroundings and responded to them by writing poetry. Some famous Romantic poets include Percy Shelley, Lord Byron, John Keats, Samuel Taylor Coleridge and William Wordsworth.

Here is a well-known poem by William Wordsworth called *Daffodils*. It was written in 1804 while he was living in the Lake District, an area of outstanding natural beauty in England.

Daffodils

I wander'd lonely as a cloud
That floats on high o'er vales and hills,
When all at once I saw a crowd,
A host of golden daffodils,
Beside the lake, beneath the trees
Fluttering and dancing in the breeze.

Continuous as the stars that shine
And twinkle on the milky way,
They stretch'd in never-ending line
Along the margin of a bay:
Ten thousand saw I at a glance
Tossing their heads in sprightly dance.

The waves beside them danced, but they
Out-did the sparkling waves in glee: –
A poet could not but be gay
In such a jocund company!
I gazed – and gazed – but little thought
What wealth the show to me had brought.

For oft, when on my couch I lie
In **vacant** or in **pensive** mood,
They flash upon that inward eye
Which is the **bliss** of **solitude**;
And then my heart with pleasure fills
And dances with the daffodils.

William Wordsworth

■ William Wordsworth, 1770–1850

■ Wordsworth was inspired by the beautiful landscapes of the Lake District. What words would you use to describe this landscape?

ACTIVITY: The Romantics

Read 'Daffodils' by William Wordsworth and complete the following tasks.

1 **Interpret** how Wordsworth feels about the landscape of the Lake District. **Identify** at least two quotes to support your answer.
2 **Identify** a word in the text which means 'cheerful and light hearted'.
3 Use a dictionary to find the definitions of the highlighted words in the poem.
4 Which verbs in the text are used to personify the daffodils? To remind yourself about what personification is, turn to page 109 in Chapter 5.
5 How do you know that the poem is based on a memory. **Identify** two pieces of evidence in the poem that shows he is looking back on an earlier experience.
6 **Analyse** how the memory of the daffodils helps the poet.
7 Using examples from the poem, **demonstrate** how effectively Wordsworth captures what is shown in the image on page 136.

In pairs, **discuss** the following:
● Are there any places you've been to that have had an impact on you? What was it about these places that you found so striking? How did your surroundings make you feel?

Now, using some of the techniques you have learnt, write a few lines or the first stanza of a poem about a place you have been inspired by.

◆ Assessment opportunities

In this activity you have practised skills that are assessed using Criterion B: Reading, Criterion C: Speaking and Criterion D: Writing.

▼ Links to: Arts – Romanticism in art

As well as giving rise to some of the greatest poets in history, the Romantic movement can also be credited for giving us some spectacular examples of visual art. Painters including John Constable, JMW Turner, Caspar David Friedrich and Francisco Goya used their paintings to capture the landscapes that inspired them. You can see an example of one of the paintings below.

Literature and art go hand in hand, and together they can provide us with a glimpse of the past. It is difficult to talk about Romantic poetry without making any reference to Romantic art!

Look again at the image above. How do you think the painter felt about the landscape they were depicting? What does the painting reveal about the relationship between humans and nature?

Do you like what you see? Why not use a search engine to carry out some research about Romantic art? Find out more about what inspired artists and how they produced their art.

Go even further and have a go at creating your own Romantic painting! Perhaps you can use the poem you wrote earlier for inspiration.

EXTENSION: POSTER POEMS

Each month, Billy Mills, a poet and small press publisher in Ireland, invites readers of *The Guardian* to write poems on a chosen theme. Mills provides an introduction to the topic, sometimes citing famous examples and then readers can share their poems by 'posting' them in the comment section, hence the title, 'poster poems'.

Prompts in the past have ranged from single words to complex ideas and have included the alphabet, change, ice, darkness and ruins. There are many more, and you can use the link below to read some examples.

www.theguardian.com/books/series/posterpoems

We'll keep the idea of writing poems based on a specific theme, but let's **interpret** the word 'poster' differently.

1 On your own, write down the first word that comes into your head on a small piece of paper. Don't share it with anyone! Fold your piece of paper over so that what you have written can't be seen.

2 Get other people in your class to do the same thing, then put your pieces of paper in a hat or tray and mix them up.

3 Take turns to pick out a piece of folded paper. Open it up and read what it says.

4 Use this word as inspiration for writing a short poem.

Present your poem using a poster. The word that inspired your poem should be clearly stated on your poster, and you should include some inspiring pictures related to your topic.

Struggling to find the words to put your poem together? Try using the technique for a 'jigsaw' poem!

Look at the words listed in the table. Take a couple of minutes to add your favourite words or phrases to the list.

Use these words to create your own poem.

evening	morning	night	swift
sun	moon	star	always
blue	yellow	purple	forever
red	orange	black	never
white	brown	green	window
rain	wind	snow	stairs
laugh	smile	cry	soaring
remember	forget	recall	graceful
dance	sing	play	door
forest	mountain	river	do
light	dark	shadows	get
storm	sea	ship	have
weak	strong	delicate	whisper
beneath	over	around	mystical
languid	spiritless	weary	shout
elated	spirited	happy	scream
in	on	to	falter
by	near	from	collapse
my	your	its	create
his	her	ours	remember
I	you	he	magical
she	it	they	imagine
slowly	quickly	lightly	delightful
water	earth	fire	tumble
who	the	a	
said	like	as	
how	when	what	
fall	spring	summer	
together	alone	apart	
mad	powerful	delirious	
vision	dream	picture	

Display your poster poems in your classroom.

How can we use poetry to express our thoughts, feelings and ideas?

As we have seen already, over the centuries writers have used poetry as a means of personal expression, as well as a way of highlighting issues of great and universal importance. Poetry has been used to challenge our existing perceptions of the world and has encouraged us to think deeply about our behaviour, both as individuals and as members of wider, even global, communities; poems can contain powerful messages, which can be utilized to change the way in which we think about the world. But just how can we convey these ideas through literary texts?

Language and the way in which we use it can help shape these messages and it is through the stylistic choices we make that we can transmit these crucial ideas. The beauty of poetry lies in its subtlety – we can use imagery to shock, move and motivate readers into thought and action and it is through **symbolism** that we can often touch upon subjects that may be deemed too dangerous to explore in any other form.

Writing poetry can also help us to better understand ourselves and our own emotions. For many writers, writing poetry can be quite therapeutic – next time you're feeling angry or frustrated, don't scream and shout, just write it out in a poem! You'll be surprised at how satisfying it can be!

And remember, you don't just have to *write* poetry to benefit from it; *reading* poetry can be an equally rewarding experience. As readers we can use poetry to express ideas or feelings when we can't find the right words ourselves.

What is a metaphor?

In Chapter 3 we looked at what a simile was – a **metaphor** is a **stylistic device** that can be used to create a similar effect.

A metaphor is a stronger method of creating **imagery** than a simile. Unlike similes, where the words 'like' or 'as' are used to compare things, metaphors allow us to say that a person, place, animal or thing IS something else, rather than just similar to it.

Metaphors don't have literal meanings, that is to say, they are not true. Writers use them to express ideas in a more subtle manner.

Let's look at an example:

She drowned in a sea of grief.

What makes this a metaphor? Why can this not be literally true? What do we learn about how the person in the sentence is feeling? Take a few minutes to discuss this with a partner or group.

There is no such thing as a sea of grief but the metaphor shows us that she is incredibly sad. Her grief is so great that is it like a sea, surrounding her from all sides and making her feel as if she is drowning. It is a more interesting way of expressing sadness, and gives us a sense of the extent of her feeling.

Look at the following examples and think about what they mean. It might help you to draw an image for each one!

1   The detective listened to her tales with a wooden face.

2   The children were roses grown in concrete gardens, beautiful and forlorn.

3   The daggers of heat pierced through his black t-shirt.

4   His teeth were pearls.

5   She broke her sister's heart.

Look through some of the poems in this chapter and see if you can find any metaphors. They can be tricky to spot!

The T.S. Eliot Prize, named after the modernist poet and founder of the Poetry Book Society, is awarded once a year for a new collection of poetry. John Burnside won the award in 2012 for his book, *Black Cat Bone*. Below he tells the *Telegraph* how poetry has changed his life.

How poetry can change lives

It's unusual for me to wake late to the sound of London traffic on a Tuesday morning, with vivid and apparently real memories of having spent a large part of the previous evening discussing the importance of poetry with other poets, journalists, radio and even television interviewers. So winning this year's TS Eliot award was as thought-provoking as it was gratifying to the ego and restorative of the bank balance.

Normally, I wake in the Fife countryside, to the sound of my neighbour's sheep and the occasional *buzzard and, on one level, that is what most of my poetry is 'about': everyday experiences, the land, the lives of other animals, the light on a certain kind of winter's day, in a specific Scottish place, the seemingly unremarkable details of the here and now. Yet whenever the question 'What does poetry do?' or 'What is it for?' is raised, I have no hesitation in replying that poetry is central to our culture, and that it is capable of being the most powerful and transformative of the arts.

There are poems that have, literally, changed my life, because they have changed the way I looked at and listened to the world; there are poems that, on repeated reading, have gradually revealed to me areas of my own experience that, for reasons both personal and societal, I had lost sight of; and there are poems that I have read over and over again, knowing they contained some secret knowledge that I had yet to discover, but refused to give up on. So, at the most basic level, poetry is important because it makes us think, it opens us up to wonder and the sometimes astonishing possibilities of language. It is, in its subtle yet powerful way, a discipline for re-engaging with a world we take too much for granted.

When the purveyors of **bottom-line** thinking call a mountain or a lake a 'natural resource', something to be merely exploited and used up, poetry reminds us that lakes and mountains are more than items on a spreadsheet; when a dictatorship imprisons and tortures its citizens, people write poems because the rhythms of poetry and the way it uses language to celebrate and to honour, rather than to **denigrate** and abuse, is **akin** to the rhythms and attentiveness of justice. Central to this attentiveness is the key ingredient of poetry, the metaphor, which Hannah Arendt defined as 'the means by which the oneness of the world is poetically brought about'. It's that power to bring things together, to unify experience as 'the music of what happens', that the best poetry achieves.

Most of us feel that this is true of the great dead poets society of history, of Shakespeare and Milton, of Coleridge and Shelley and, of course, of TS Eliot, an American who re-envisioned and so renewed and enriched our idea of England. Yet I would argue that poetry is, or can be, as central to our experience now as it has ever been. To read 'I Am Your Waiter Tonight And My Name Is Dmitri', by the great contemporary American poet, Robert Hass, at the height of George W Bush's xenophobic repudiation of 'Old Europe', was to be reminded not just of the injustice and futility of war, but also of the very richness and complexity of history that Bush sought to **expunge**.

The Wisconsin poet Nick Lantz's collection, We Don't Know We Don't Know, brings together the natural history of Pliny the Elder and the **wittering** of Donald Rumsfeld to extraordinary effect, forcing us to ask questions about how our vision of the world and our political attitudes are manipulated by the powers that be. Apparently personal, apolitical lyrics by Lucie Brock-Broido, say, or Alan Shapiro make us think again about the dynamics of our day-to-day relationships with other creatures, from **spouses** and children to the wild things that we keep forgetting are out there, where the suburban garden or the porch light ends.

All of these poets **insinuate** their way into our lives with their music and wit, but they stay on to make us think again about how we live and what we are capable of – just as poets have always done. Poets today are as challenging, both of public life and private accommodations, as Andrew Marvell was when he gently confronted Oliver Cromwell's foreign policy in his 'An Horatian Ode Upon Cromwell's Return from Ireland'; or, in more intimately reflective mode, TS Eliot was, when he drew together and made immediate essential philosophical ideas about the basic facts of life – time, place, endurance, the difficult disciplines of love – in the Four Quartets. As much as it has ever done, poetry renews and deepens the gift that most surely makes us human: the imagination. And that is as essential to public as it is to private life, because the more imaginative we are, the more compassionate we become – and that, surely, is the highest **virtue** of all.

ℹ *buzzard – a large type of bird of prey similar to a hawk and a vulture

CONNECT–EXTEND–CHALLENGE

ATL

Communication skills: Read critically and for comprehension

Read the text on page 140 and answer the questions that follow.

Task 1

Look at the words highlighted in the text and match each one with a synonym from the list below.

abolish	belittle	disapproval
fundamental	honour	imply
partners	rambling	similar

Read the text again and highlight ten of your own words or phrases. Use www.thesaurus.com to help you find synonyms for your chosen vocabulary.

Use a word cloud generator of your choice to record the vocabulary for the text.

Task 2

1 Why has the poet woken up to the sound of London traffic?
2 **Identify** how you know that he has received some money for winning the prize. Find some evidence to support your answer.
3 What does Burnside say his poetry is about?
4 **Identify** the stylistic device he thinks is one of the most important components of poetry. **Interpret** why he feels this way. Do you agree?
5 In your own words, **explain** how poetry has changed his life and this way of thinking. Find at least five reasons and don't forget to support your answer with evidence from the text.
- How are the ideas and information presented CONNECTED to what you already knew?
- What new ideas did you get that EXTENDED or pushed your thinking in new direction?
- What is still challenging or confusing you? What questions do you have now?

◆ Assessment opportunities

In this activity you have practised skills that are assessed using Criterion B: Reading.

■ War photographers changed how people accessed images of conflict, particularly from the First World War onwards. Photographs provide valuable evidence for moments that have otherwise been missed from the history of the war

Poems are a fantastic way of raising awareness about issues of global significance but can be an equally great tool for critiquing things that we are strongly opposed to. Through poems we can gain a voice through which we can criticize the way certain governments or authorities behave or act; sometimes we can use language to simply vent our frustration about things that may be beyond our control. Either way, it can be a writer's way of making a difference, no matter how small.

War Photographer

In his dark room he is finally alone
with spools of suffering set out in ordered rows.
The only light is red and softly glows,
as though this were a church and he
a priest preparing to intone a Mass.
Belfast. Beirut. Phnom Penh. All flesh is grass.

He has a job to do. Solutions slop in trays
beneath his hands, which did not tremble then
though seem to now. Rural England. Home again
to ordinary pain which simple weather can dispel,
to fields which don't explode beneath the feet
of running children in a nightmare heat.

Something is happening. A stranger's features
faintly start to twist before his eyes,
a half-formed ghost. He remembers the cries
of this man's wife, how he sought approval
without words to do what someone must
and how the blood stained into foreign dust.

A hundred agonies in black and white
from which his editor will pick out five or six
for Sunday's supplement. The reader's eyeballs prick
with tears between the bath and pre-lunch beers.
From the aeroplane he stares impassively at where
he earns his living and they do not care.

Carol Ann Duffy

▼ Links to: Individuals and societies – History and Geography; Science – photography

When photography was first introduced in the nineteenth century, it changed our way of recording history.

Today, with developments in camera technology and digital communication, photography allows us to use images to capture time, place and people and share them in a matter of minutes. Never has the world seemed smaller and more real than in the age of digital photography.

Photographs have changed the way we see the world and allow us to see the real impact of events taking place across the globe on our planet and other communities.

In groups ...

• Research industries that have been revolutionized by digital photography and its technology.

• Choose a period of time you have studied and search for images that give an insight into that period of time or event.

• Find out about the history of photography and photojournalism.

Choose a format and/or a platform to present your work to the class.

ACTIVITY: Capturing essence – 'War Photographer'

Task 1

In pairs, **evaluate** whether 'War Photographer' by Carol Ann Duffy, falls into this category of poems that are written to make a difference.

Read the poem and complete the tasks that follow:

1 **Interpret** the attitudes Duffy is expressing in the poem.
2 **Summarise** each stanza using a single sentence.
3 **Analyse** how Duffy uses language and stylistic features to present these attitudes. Choose some examples from the text and copy and complete the table below.

Task 2

1 In pairs, **discuss** some other important issues which you feel strongly about. If you get stuck, here are some suggestions:
   - conflict/war/refugees
   - poverty/hunger/homelessness
   - environmental problems/animal rights
   - human rights issues.
2 Choose one of these issues and express your thoughts, feelings or ideas through writing a poem. Try to include as many of the techniques we have explored in this chapter.
3 Give your poem a title which highlights the most important issue your poem addresses.

Example from poem (quote)	Language feature/literary technique	Meaning/effect
Example: 'Belfast. Beirut. Phnom Penh.'	Proper nouns	She uses proper nouns to show us that the horrors captured on camera by the photographer are very real and take place in real places, across the world.

4 Duffy effectively gets her point across. **Evaluate** how successfully she uses imagery to help her do this.
5 Choose one image that you find particularly striking and use it to create a picture. **Explain** the effect this image might have on readers.

How can we use poems to tell stories?

A poem can be a surprisingly good way to tell a story. In fact some of the oldest stories we know were told using poetry! A poem that tells a story is known as a narrative poem. Like stories, narrative poems can include a number of different characters and the story can be told through their voices or that of a single narrator. The length of a narrative poem can vary and some are as long as novels, while others are relatively short.

There are lots and lots of famous examples, including *Beowulf, Paradise Lost,* and *The Raven*, which we looked at briefly earlier in this chapter.

Find out more about these poems and other examples of **narrative poetry**.

Nonsense poetry, as you would expect from its name, is poetry that doesn't always seem to make sense! This might be because it contains made up words or because it puts existing words in unusual contexts. Nonsense poetry can be used to describe absurd or comical situations and is generally lighthearted. The tone is usually helped by a simple rhyme scheme. Most, but not all, nonsense poetry is written for the amusement of young children, and writers including Roald Dahl, Dr. Seuss and Lewis Carroll can all take credit for some of the most memorable examples of the genre.

Edward Lear is another English poet who dabbled in nonsense verse, and it is Lear who is responsible for creating one of the best known nonsense poems in literature, *The Owl and the Pussy-cat*, which as it happens, is also a narrative poem!

■ The characters from Lear's much loved poem

The Owl and the Pussy-cat

The Owl and the Pussy-cat went to sea
In a beautiful pea-green boat:
They took some honey, and plenty of money
Wrapped up in a five-pound note.
The Owl looked up to the stars above,
And sang to a small guitar,
'O lovely Pussy, O Pussy, my love,
What a beautiful Pussy you are,
You are,
You are!
What a beautiful Pussy you are!'

Pussy said to the Owl, 'You elegant fowl,
How charmingly sweet you sing!
Oh! let us be married; too long we have tarried,
But what shall we do for a ring?'
They sailed away, for a year and a day,
To the land where the bong-tree grows;
And there in a wood a Piggy-wig stood,
With a ring at the end of his nose,
His nose,
His nose,
With a ring at the end of his nose.

'Dear Pig, are you willing to sell for one shilling
Your ring?' Said the Piggy, 'I will.'
So they took it away, and were married next day
By the turkey who lives on the hill.
They dined on mince and slices of quince,
Which they ate with a runcible spoon;
And hand in hand, on the edge of the sand,
They danced by the light of the moon,
The moon,
The moon,
They danced by the light of the moon.

Edward Lear

ACTIVITY: What nonsense!

■ ATL

Communication skills: Use appropriate forms of writing for different purposes and audiences; structure information in summaries, essays and reports

Creative-thinking skills: Create original works and ideas; use existing works and ideas in new ways

Read the Edward Lear poem and complete the tasks which follow:

1 **Identify** the target audience for this poem. Explain why and give evidence to support your answer.
2 **Summarise** the story told in the poem in a few sentences.
3 Keeping in mind a possible target audience, **use** the poem to create your own multimodal text. Create a storyboard or comic strip in which you can **use** both words and pictures to tell the story. Try changing the poetry into prose for this activity.

After you have created your storyboard or comic, in pairs or groups of three, **discuss** what you think is the more effective way of telling the story. Poetry or prose? What do you think would engage young children more? Make sure you can **justify** your ideas.

◆ Assessment opportunities

In this activity you have practised skills that are assessed using Criterion B: Reading and Criterion D: Writing.

ACTIVITY: Jabberwocky

Lewis Carroll loved a bit of nonsense! He includes several narrative poems in his novel *Through the Looking Glass,* the sequel to *Alice's Adventures in Wonderland.* One of these poems is 'Jabberwocky'.

Task 1

Watch the short clip of the Mad Hatter reciting 'Jabberwocky'.

www.youtube.com/watch?v=b0dhJXUX6I4

When you have finished watching the clip, think about trying to represent or capture the essence of the poem. To do this, choose:

- **a colour**
- **a symbol**
- **an image.**

With a partner or group, share your colour, symbol and image. Give reasons for your choices.

Task 2

Answer the following questions:

- **Why does Alice interrupt him at the start?**
- **What is the poem about?**
- **What is unusual about it?**

In pairs, look at the opening stanza of the poem:

> `Twas brillig, and the slithy toves
> Did gyre and gimble in the wabe:
> All mimsy were the borogoves,
> And the mome raths outgrabe

Identify which word classes the underlined words belong to. To help you, we've used a different colour for each word class! Make sure you can justify your choice.

Stuck? Maybe this will help …

- **Interpret** the function of the word – does it show an action? Is it describing something? Do we know anything about time or place?
- **Analyse** what the words might mean.

Once you think you've classified all of the words correctly, use a search engine to check your answers and help you find out the actual meaning of the nonsense words in the poem. They are all made up by Lewis Carroll!

Now that you know what the words mean, it's time to explore the deeper meaning of the poem. Have a go at completing the following tasks. Try to find evidence to support your answers.

1 **Identify** the atmosphere that has been created.
2 **Analyse** how the strange animals are feeling this afternoon.
3 **Discuss** how the stanza might fit with the rest of the poem. **Identify** its purpose.

■ The strange creatures from Carroll's poem. Which ones can you identify from the poem?

Does the way in which we share and write poems vary from place to place?

HOW CAN WE USE POETRY TO MAKE CONNECTIONS WITH OTHERS?

Poetry has the power to bring people closer together; through poetry we can travel the world without the need to leave the comfort of our homes! Each place has its own, unique identity and that identity can be shared through the music and language of poetry.

Poetry is a global phenomenon. Each country has its own tradition of poetry, whether oral or written, cultivated over centuries. Poems can allow us to gain a meaningful insight into another culture, another way of life. Through reading poems from other places, even if it is in translation, we can learn to understand others better and reflect on the similarities that bind us together as people.

The essence of a place is reflected in the very structure of the poetry that comes out of it. It can be found in the words and between the lines, inside the rhythm and the rhyme of every verse. In some places the poems have been transformed completely over time, while in others, traditional forms are held on to and preserved, as reminders of times past.

One of the great things about exploring new places and being exposed to new forms of poetry, is that you can 'borrow' or learn new ideas.

■ The beginning of a poem on the calligraphy composed by Qiyam al-Din Muhammad al-hasan, who worked in the Persian city of Qazwin

The **ghazals** of India and Pakistan are deeply rooted in a greater tradition of poetry, which came from the Middle East and North Africa, while the **sonnet**, which can be found across Europe, originated in Italy in the thirteenth century.

The Pakistani poet, Muhammed Iqbal, was said to have been influenced by the British Romantics and many poets, who formed part of a movement known as imagism in the early twentieth century, drew inspiration from the **haiku** poems of Japan. American writer Adrienne Rich has written many ghazals of her own but doesn't always follow the strict structure of the traditional form. After all, in poetry we're allowed to break the rules once in a while!

THINK–PAIR–SHARE

What is the poetry from your home country like? Is it very similar to some of the British and American poems we have looked at in this chapter? Does it have a specific structure? How is poetry shared in your culture?

Discuss your thoughts with a partner and then share with the rest of the class.

ACTIVITY: Poetic borrowing

Carry out some research about the highlighted words on page 147. See if you can find a definition and example for each one. Can you find any other poems that are specific to a particular place? Perhaps you can find some writers who have 'borrowed' ideas from poems from other places or cultures?

Task 1

In pairs or groups of three **discuss** the following. Make sure you can **justify** your ideas.

- **What do you think of sharing poetry from different places?**
- **Identify** how we might benefit from this kind of sharing.
- Can you think of any negative consequences of sharing or 'borrowing'?
- **Evaluate** whether the message of a poem can be lost in translation.
- **Analyse** the differences in layout, conventions and stylistic choices.

Task 2

Question starts

Brainstorm a list of at least 12 questions about the poetic borrowing. Use these question-starts to help you think of interesting questions:

Why …? How would it be different if …? What are the reasons …? Suppose that …? What if …? What if we knew …? What is the purpose of …? What would change if …?

Review the brainstormed list and star the questions that seem most interesting. Then, select one or more of the starred questions to discuss for a few moments.

Reflect: What new ideas do you have about the topic, concept or object that you didn't have before?

◆ Assessment opportunities

In this activity you have practised skills that are assessed using Criterion B: Reading and Criterion C: Speaking.

Should we still read poetry today?

WHAT CAN WE GAIN FROM READING POETRY?

Throughout this chapter we have looked at what poetry can add to our lives, whether we write our own, or just enjoy reading the work of others. While to many of us the benefits of reading poetry are obvious and indisputable, there are others out there who are still skeptical and question whether there is room for poetry in our lives today. Why do schools still teach us how to read, write and interpret poetry? Surely it would be more worthwhile to spend that time perfecting more practical skills, like essay writing?

But reading poetry *is* worthwhile and it is crucial that we keep this age old tradition alive in our busy, technology obsessed world! Aside from making us more mindful and socially aware, poetry furnishes us with many useful skills – it teaches us to communicate articulately, in fewer words; it develops our critical-thinking skills by forcing us to look for deeper meanings, to read between the lines, to make inferences; reading poetry makes us more

■ *The muse of poetry* by Dutch painter Willem Basse – 1634

knowledgeable about issues that we might never have encountered in other areas of our lives; it places before us the universal power of literature to bring people closer together.

What have you gained from reading poetry in this chapter? Why do you think it is important that we still read poetry today?

I used to think, now I think

■ **ATL**

Reflection skills: Consider content

Creative-thinking skills: Practise visible thinking strategies and techniques

When we began this chapter on poetry, we all had some initial ideas on what it was all about. In just a few sentences, write what it is that you used to think about poetry. Take a minute to think back and then write down your response to 'I used to think …'

Now, think about how your ideas about poetry have changed as a result of what we have been doing in the tasks. Again, in just a few sentences write down what you now think about poetry. Start your sentences with, 'But now, I think …'

In pairs, share and **explain** how your thoughts have changed.

◆ Assessment opportunities

In this activity you have practised skills that are assessed using Criterion D: Writing.

Pay with a poem: coffee for poetry deal spreads around the globe

Poetry will become the new currency in coffee outlets around the world for a day as World Poetry Day campaign spreads to 34 countries

Annoyed at the rising price of your coffee, and a hipsterisation so extreme that it's apparently become a symbol of gentrification? Offended at your barista for not rewarding your loyalty with a free latte? You can forget it all on Monday and put your literary talent to use instead, by exchanging a handwritten poem for coffee in 1,280 outlets around the world.

To mark World Poetry Day on 21 March, an Austrian coffee roasting company is offering a shot of caffeine to customers who hand in a poem. More than 100,000 people gobbled up the offer last year according to coffee company Julius Meinl. The firm has now expanded it from 23 into 34 countries, mostly in central and eastern Europe, but also including locations in London, Edinburgh, the US, Canada and Australia. You can find a map of this year's participating establishments here.

Poet and conceptual artist Robert Montgomery will mark the occasion by collecting up all the public contributions and turning them into an art installation in a secret London location.

ACTIVITY: Pay your way with a poem!

■ **ATL**

Communication skills: Write for different purposes

Imagine a world where you can pay for things with poems instead of money! Well, in 2015 an Austrian coffee roasting company tried to create exactly that!

Read the article from *the Guardian* and complete the tasks that follow:

1 **Identify** how the writer engages the readers in the opening paragraph.
2 **Evaluate** the effect of the phrase 'gobbled up'.

3 Did a coffee shop near you participate? Follow the link below to find out!
www.meinlcoffee.com/poetry/campaigns/pay-with-a-poem-2016/#poem-location-map
4 What would you write about to get a free coffee? In pairs, brainstorm some ideas.
5 **Discuss** how you would feel about living in a world where we paid each other in poems rather than money.
6 Write a poem about a world without money.

◆ Assessment opportunities

In this activity you have practised skills that are assessed using Criterion D: Writing.

ACTIVITY: Can a computer write poetry?

Are we approaching an age where eventually poetry will be written by machines? Let's hope not! But an interesting idea to ponder nonetheless.

Watch the video and listen to Oscar Schwartz talk about whether computers can write poetry or not. You can listen to the talk with subtitles and/or read the transcript to help you follow it more easily.

www.ted.com/talks/oscar_schwartz_can_a_computer_write_poetry

Complete the tasks below:

1 **Identify** where Schwartz obtained the idea to study whether computers could write poetry.
2 **Identify** what inspired him to use then create a poetry online test. What is the test called?
3 **Evaluate** the results obtained by the test.
4 What was Gertrude Stein able to do?
5 **State** what percentage of the audience correctly identified the poem written by the computer.
6 **Summarise** Schwartz's point of view after gathering all the results.

In pairs, or groups of three, **discuss** the following:

- **Identify** what it is that makes poetry, or any form of art, human.
- Does the meaning of poetry come from the reader, the author, or both?
- What makes good poetry?
- **Discuss** whether Artificial Intelligence can ever experience human-like emotions.

◆ Assessment opportunities

In this activity you have practised skills that are assessed using Criterion A: Listening and Criterion C: Speaking.

❗ Take action

Poetry is a powerful tool to express ourselves, but what can you do with the poems you have written? There is so much technology that you can use to showcase your poetry.

- ❗ Click on the link below for top tips on using multimedia to enhance your poems:

  www.powerpoetry.org/resources/multimedia-poetry

- ❗ Take part in poetry competitions, there is something for everyone and you can decide on the level that best suits you.

- ❗ World Poetry Day is celebrated on 21 March. Through this celebration UNESCO recognizes that people around the world share the same feelings, questions and common humanity.

- ❗ Look at the quote below on poetry from Irina Bokova, Director-General of UNESCO:

  'By paying tribute to the men and women whose only instrument is free speech, who imagine and act, UNESCO recognizes in poetry its value as a symbol of the human spirit's creativity. By giving form and words to that which has none – such as the unfathomable beauty that surrounds us, the immense suffering and misery of the world – poetry contributes to the expansion of our common humanity, helping to increase its strength, solidarity and self-awareness.'

- ❗ Click on the link to explore further what this day is about and make notes:

  www.un.org/en/events/poetryday/

- ❗ In groups, brainstorm ideas on how your school can be part of World Poetry Day!

SOME SUMMATIVE TASKS TO TRY

Use these tasks to apply and extend your learning in this chapter. These tasks are designed so that you can evaluate your learning in the Language Acquisition Criteria.

THIS TASK CAN BE USED TO EVALUATE YOUR LEARNING IN CRITERION C TO PROFICIENT LEVEL

Task 1: Interactive oral

Choose a poet from your country or culture, or one who writes in your mother tongue.

Using the internet and other sources, carry out some research about the poet and prepare a presentation about them and their writing.

You will engage in a discussion with the teacher on poetry.

■ You are expected to speak for 4–5 minutes.

You might want to use this website for some of your research: **www.poetryarchive.org**.

In your presentation you should include the following:
■ A brief biography of the poet, including where they are from and which language they write in.
■ The themes explored in their poetry.
■ What inspires them to write.
■ An example of their work – you can choose a particular poem to focus on. **Summarize** the content of the poem, explain what inspired it and select a few lines to talk about in more depth. You may have to do some translating here for your audience!

THIS TASK CAN BE USED TO EVALUATE YOUR LEARNING IN CRITERION A TO PROFICIENT LEVEL

Task 2: Ways to speak English

■ View the website and watch the video and answer the following questions.
■ Use your own words as much as possible.
■ Do not use translating devices or dictionaries for this task.
■ You have 60 minutes to complete this task.

Video: **www.ted.com/talks/jamila_lyiscott_3_ways_to_speak_english?language=en**

Questions

1 **Identify** literary features used by Jamila.   (strand i)
2 **Evaluate** the tone of the text.   (strand ii)
3 What does the tone of the text tell us about the meaning and the speaker's attitude towards language?   (strand ii)
4 Give reasons for Jamila's argument on Standard English.   (strand i)
5 **Identify** the examples that highlight the difference between dialect and Standard English.   (strand i)
6 **Evaluate** what Standard English means to you.   (strand iii)
7 **Identify** the word that Jamila uses instead of 'language'. Why does she use this word?   (strand i)
8 Provide a list of words or an extract from the text: Why has the speaker used these words?   (strand ii)
9 Who is the audience? What has the speaker done to get the interest of the listeners?   (strand ii)
10 How has this text influenced your ideas or feelings about language, history and identity?   (strand iii)
11 Do you agree with Jamila? Why? Why not?   (strand iii)
12 **Interpret** if this text is poetry. Make connections with your own experience of language and identity.   (strand iii)

THIS TASK CAN BE USED TO EVALUATE YOUR LEARNING IN CRITERION D TO PROFICIENT LEVEL

Task 3: Writing

- Time allowed: You have 60 minutes to complete the task.
- This task will be completed in class under supervision.
- 'What is the value of poetry?' **Discuss**.
- Task: Write an essay of 300–400 words. Include your own personal experience and what you have learnt in this chapter to support your point of view.

Reflection

In this chapter we have explored the **conventions** of poetry and have even had a go at writing our own. As part of this process we have developed our knowledge of the **stylistic choices** that writers make so that they are able to convey particular **messages** to their intended audience. In addition, we have considered the powerful impact that poetry can have on our lives and how it can be used for **personal and cultural expression** as well as a way to make **connections** with others.

Use this table to reflect on your own learning in this chapter.					
Questions we asked		Answers we found	Any further questions now?		
Factual: What is a poem? What are the conventions of a poem?					
Conceptual: Why do we write poetry? How can we use poetry to express our thoughts, feelings and ideas? Does the way in which we share and write poems vary from place to place? How can we use poetry to create music with words? How can we use poems to tell stories?					
Debatable: Why does poetry matter? Should we still read poetry today? To what extent do words empower us? How does poetry mirror what it means to be human?					
Approaches to learning you used in this chapter:		Description – what new skills did you learn?	How well did you master the skills?		
			Novice	Learner	Practitioner	Expert
Communication skills						
Reflection skills						
Critical-thinking skills						
Creative-thinking skills						
Transfer skills						
Learner profile attribute(s)		Reflect on the importance of being knowledgeable for your learning in this chapter.			
Knowledgeable					

Glossary

adjective Word used to describe an object or a person; also called 'describing words'

adverb Word that describes a verb, giving more information about an action

alliteration The repetition of sounds in a sentence or a line

antonym A word that means the opposite of another word in the same language

idiom An expression, usually specific to a particular culture or language, which means something different from its literal meaning

imperative Can refer to verbs or sentences which are used to give commands or instructions

interrogative sentence A sentence which asks a question; ends with a question mark

metaphor A literary technique which allows us to say that a person, place, animal or thing IS something else, rather than just similar to it

modal auxiliary verb A 'helping' verb that can be used to alter the tone of a sentence and indicates likelihood, ability, permission, and obligation

multimodal texts Texts which consist of more than one mode, for instance texts which make use of both written and visual modes

narrative A story or account of events

noun A person, place, or thing

onomatopoeia Words which create or represent sounds

paragraph A series of sentences grouped together and linked by a common topic; found in **prose**

personification A literary technique used to give inanimate objects or concepts human characteristics

prose Written or spoken language presented in an ordinary way

rhetorical question A question used for literary effect which does not require an answer

repetition This refers to the repetition of words or grammatical structures for emphasis or to create a desired effect

simile A simile is a way of describing something by comparing it to something else, often using the word 'like' or 'as'

sobriquet A nickname

stanza An arrangement of lines used to organize and divide the structure of a poem; also known as **verse**

stylistic device Language and techniques used to create specific effects in literary and non-literary texts

synonym A word that means exactly or nearly the same as another word in the same language

syntax The arrangement or order of words or phrases within a sentence

verb A word which expresses an action, occurrence or state of being

Acknowledgements

Photo credits

p.2 *t* © Lightwise/123RF; *b* © Ammentorp/123RF; **p.4** © Moviestore Collection/REX/Shutterstock; **p.7** *tl* © PCN Photography/Alamy Stock Photo, *tr* © Geoffrey Robinson/Alamy Stock Photo, *bl* © Robertharding/Alamy Stock Photo, *br* © PF-(sdasm2)/Alamy Stock Photo; **p.9** © AF archive/Alamy Stock Photo; **p.10** © Rick Laverty/123RF; **p.17** © Ion Chiosea/123RF; **p.22** *l* © Cathy Yeulet/123RF, *r* © Ian Allenden/123RF; **p.23** © Ilja Mašík – Fotolia, © arsdigital – Fotolia, © karelnoppe/Shutterstock, © LuckyImages/Shutterstock.com; **p.26-7** © kudryashka/123RF; **p.30** *t* © Dave Broberg/123RF, *l* © Dmitrii Kiselev/123RF, *r* © Pazargic Liviu/123RF, *b* © Wavebreak Media Ltd/123RF; **p.31** © fuchs-photography/iStock/Thinkstock; **p.32** © Igor Yaruta/123RF; **p.34** © Monkey Business/Fotolia; **p.36** *l* © Mikhail Pogosov/123RF, *c* kuco/123RF, *r* © GP Library Limited/Alamy Stock Photo; **p.37** *l* © Library of Congress, Prints and Photographic Division [LC-USZ6-2003], *r* © Library of Congress, Prints and Photographic Division [LC-USZ62-131335]; **p.42** © Peter Cade/The Image Bank/Getty Images; **p.43** *t* © Skynesher/E+/Getty Images, *c* © Viacheslav Nikolaienko/123RF, *b* © Fuse/Corbis/Getty Images; **p.44** © paylessimages/123RF.com; **p.48-9** © Belchonock/123RF; **p.49** *t* © cokemomo/123RF, *c* © Katarzyna BiaÅasiewicz/123RF, *b* © liza5450/123RF; **p.50** *t* © Paul Grecaud/123RF, *ct* © Joerg Hackemann/123RF, *cb* © Dmitry Pichugin/Fotolia, *b* © Nick Gregory/Alamy Stock Photo; **p.51** *t* © Images By Kenny/Alamy Stock Photo, *ct* © Boaz Rottem/Alamy Stock Photo, *cb* © Heinz Leitner/123RF, *b* © Ingram Publishing Company/Ultimate Food Photography; **p.52** © BWAC Images/Alamy Stock Photo, **p.54** *l* © Gustavo Caballero/Getty Images Entertainment, *r* © LUNA/Alamy Stock Photo; **p.55** © egal/iStock/Thinkstock/Getty Images; **p.56** *l* © Feverpitched/123RF, *r* © Shannon Fagan/123RF; **p.57** *l* © Iulia Iun/123RF, *r* © Wong Sze Yuen/123RF; **p.59** © World History Archive/TopFoto; **p.60** *t* © Rich-Joseph Facun/Getty Images, *ct* © David Bathgate/Corbis News/Getty Images, *cb* © Cathy Yeulet/123RF, *b* © Wong Yu Liang/123RF; **p.62** *t* © stuporter/Fotolia, *c* © Rattanapon Muanpimthong/123RF; **p.63** © Alexander Mychko/123RF; **p.65** © Oxfam America; **p.68** © World Food Programme, 2019; **p.72** © Georgejmclittle/123RF; **p.73** © Volodymyr Krasyuk/123RF; **p.74** © lightpoet – Fotolia; **p.75** © redsnapper/Alamy Stock Photo; **p.76** © SAOF; **p.77** *t* © Ronnachai Limpakdeesavasd/123RF, *b* © Andrew Fox/Alamy Stock Photo; **p.79** *both* © Pictorial Press Ltd/Alamy Stock Photo; **p.80** *t* © Johan Möllerberg/123RF, *b* © CPC Collection/Alamy Stock Photo; **p.81** © North Wind Picture Archives/Alamy Stock Photo; **p.82** *t* © Cameron/Julia Margaret/Library of Congress, *b* © Mario Tama/Getty Images News; **p.83** © Granger Historical Picture Archve/Alamy Stock Photo; **p.84** *t* © dpa picture alliance/Alamy Stock Photo, *bl* © Delmas Lehman/123RF, *br* © Nature Picture Library/Alamy Stock Photo; **p.88** © robertharding/Alamy Stock Photo; **p.91** © Francisco de Casa Gonzalez/123RF; **p.94** © albertobogo/Fotolia; **p.96** © SAOF; **p.98** © Alfio Scisetti/123RF; **p.99** © ankya/123RF; **p.100** © Michael Spring/123RF; **p.101** *l* © Fine Art Images/Heritage Images/TopFoto, *r* © Jonny White/Alamy Stock Photo; **p.115** © TopFoto; **p.117** *l* © War posters/Alamy Stock Photo, *r* Library of Congress, Print and Photographuc division [LC-USZC2-1588]; **p.119** © Linda Steward/E+/Getty Images; **p.126** © Sergey Melnikov/123RF; **p.127** © Culture Club/Hulton Archive/Getty Images; **p.130** © Lebrecht Music and Arts Photo Library/Alamy Stock Photo; **p.131** © Fine Art Images/Fine Art Images; **p.132** *t* © Travel Pictures/Alamy Stock Photo, *b* © Gary Doak/Alamy Stock Photo; **p.134** *l* © Heritage Images/Hulton Archive/Getty Images, *r* © ClassicStock/TopFoto; **p.135** *l-r* © Tithi Luadthong/123RF, © Maksim Gorbunov/123RF, © andesign101/123RF, © Maksim Gorbunov/123RF, © Tithi Luadthong/123RF, © Boyan Dimitrov/123RF; **p.136** *l* © North Wind Picture Archives/Alamy Stock Photo, *r* © Jon Sparks/Alamy Stock Photo; **p.137** © PHAS/Universal Images Group/REX/Shutterstock; **p.142** © Rafael Ben-Ari/123RF; **p.144** © Lebrecht Music and Arts Photo Library/Alamy Stock Photo; **p.146** © AF Fotografie/Alamy Stock Photo; **p.147** © World History Archive/Alamy Stock Photo; **p.149** © National Gallery of Art, Washington.

t = top, *l* = left, *r* = right, *c* = centre, *b* = bottom

Text credits

p.33 'That's What I Call Home' Words and Music by Michael Kosser, Richard Mainegra, Blake Shelton © 2001, Reproduced by permission of Gosnell Music Group,Sony/Atv Tree Publishing, London W1F 9LD; **p.35** My Family's Fond of Gadgets copyright © 2014 Kenn Nesbitt. All Rights Reserved; **p.39** 'That's fascinating Grandad, but… One in three children admit they don't want to hear their relatives talk about the old days'. Copyright © The Daily Mail; **p.86** The Incredible Journey by Sheila Burnford. Published by Vintage. Permission cleared through David Higham; **p.107** Debrett's Art of Letter Writing. Copyright Debrett's Limited; **p.120** Reproduced courtesy of www.ATechnologySociety.co.uk - advice on the safety of technology and its effect on society; **p.123** Dear pen pal: how writing letters to strangers is making a comeback. Copyright Guardian News & Media Ltd 2016; **p.132** The Warm and the Cold by Ted Hughes. © Faber&Faber; **p.140** How poetry can change lives by John Burnside © Copyright Telegraph Media Group Limited; **p.142** 'War Photographer' from *Standing Female Nude* by Carol Ann Duffy. Published by Anvil Press Poetry, 1985. Copyright © Carol Ann Duffy. Reproduced by permission of the author c/o Rogers, Coleridge & White Ltd., 20 Powis Mews, London W11 1JN; **p.150** Pay with a poem: cafes around the world to exchange coffee for poetry by Marta Bausells. Copyright Guardian News & Media Ltd 2016.

Visible Thinking – ideas, framework, protocol and thinking routines – from Project Zero at the Harvard Graduate School of Education have been used in many of our activities. You can find out more here: www.visiblethinkingpz.org